LGBTQ Issues

LGBTQ Rights and Activism

Stephen Currie

ReferencePoint Press
San Diego, CA

© 2021 ReferencePoint Press, Inc.
Printed in the United States

For more information, contact:
ReferencePoint Press, Inc.
PO Box 27779
San Diego, CA 92198
www.ReferencePointPress.com

ALL RIGHTS RESERVED.
No part of this work covered by the copyright hereon may be reproduced or used in any form or by any means—graphic, electronic, or mechanical, including photocopying, recording, taping, web distribution, or information storage retrieval systems—without the written permission of the publisher.

LIBRARY OF CONGRESS CATALOGING-IN-PUBLICATION DATA

Names: Currie, Stephen, 1960- author.
Title: LGBTQ rights and activism / by Stephen Currie.
Description: San Diego : ReferencePoint Press, 2020. | Series: LGBTQ issues
 | Includes bibliographical references and index.
Identifiers: LCCN 2020011905 (print) | LCCN 2020011906 (ebook) | ISBN
 9781682829172 (library binding) | ISBN 9781682829189 (ebook)
Subjects: LCSH: Gay liberation movement--United States--History--Juvenile
 literature. | Gay rights--United States--History--Juvenile literature. |
 Gays--United States--Juvenile literature. | Lesbians--United
 States--Juvenile literature. | Bisexuals--United States--Juvenile
 literature. | Transgender people--United States--Juvenile literature.
Classification: LCC HQ76.8.U5 C87 2020 (print) | LCC HQ76.8.U5 (ebook) |
 DDC 306.76/80973--dc23
LC record available at https://lccn.loc.gov/2020011905
LC ebook record available at https://lccn.loc.gov/2020011906

Contents

Introduction   4
The LGBTQ Rights Movement

Chapter One   8
Toward Tolerance

Chapter Two   19
The AIDS Crisis

Chapter Three   30
The Struggle for Acceptance

Chapter Four   41
Transgender Issues

Chapter Five   52
Moving Forward

Source Notes	63
A Time Line of LGBTQ Rights and Activism	68
Organizations and Websites	70
For Further Research	72
Index	74
Picture Credits	79
About the Author	80

Introduction

The LGBTQ Rights Movement

For almost all of American history, transgender individuals—those who identify with a different gender than they were assigned at birth—were not permitted to serve in the military. Any openly transgender person who tried to enlist would be immediately turned away. Any member of the armed forces who wanted to transition to a different gender would be automatically discharged. There were several reasons for the ban, including concern about the effect of transgender people on troop morale and a fear that being transgender qualified as a form of mental illness. As late as 2015 the military was closed to anyone who was transgender.

New Rules Adopted and Then Rescinded

In 2016, though, then-president Barack Obama changed this policy. For the first time, members of the armed services could be open about being transgender. They could transition to a different gender while keeping their jobs and continuing to assist in America's military efforts. Before long the policy was revised to allow transgender people to join the military as well. Coming only a few years after the military began accepting openly gay and lesbian recruits, these policy changes represented something new and groundbreaking in American history. The new rules were inclusive and nondiscriminatory, and advocates for LGBTQ rights were delighted.

But their enthusiasm was short lived. Donald Trump, who succeeded Obama as president, did not support Obama's policy on transgender individuals in the military, and soon after coming to office in 2017, he announced his intention to overturn it. "The United States Government," he wrote, "will not accept or allow transgender individuals to serve in any capacity in the U.S. Military."[1] Thus, even as transgender Americans were signing up for the armed forces, the military was making preparations to dismiss them. In the spring of 2019, the Trump administration implemented a new policy regarding transgender troops. The new rule, as Trump had threatened, banned transgender people from joining the military and made it impossible for people already in the service to transition if they had not done so already.

The limitations on transgender troops have not proved popular. Studies suggest that a majority of Americans in virtually every state approves of allowing transgender people to serve in the military.

In the spring of 2019, President Donald Trump announced the implementation of a new policy that banned transgender people from joining or serving in the military.

> "There is no medically valid reason . . . to exclude transgender individuals from military service."[2]
>
> —Statement of the American Medical Association

The leaders of each branch of the armed forces have noted that transgender people do not interfere with military operations in any way. Nor does the medical establishment agree with the new policy. On the contrary, the American Medical Association, along with several other influential medical groups, has strongly opposed the ban. The American Medical Association has objected particularly to the idea that transgender people suffer from mental illness. "There is no medically valid reason . . . to exclude transgender individuals from military service,"[2] the organization wrote in a statement issued in 2019.

Activism and Rights

Transgender troops and their allies have fought back against the Trump administration policy with lawsuits and proposed legislation. Several members of Congress have introduced bills de-

The Meaning of LGBTQ

The term *LGBTQ* is a shorthand way to describe people who are not heterosexual or whose gender identity is not the gender they were assigned at birth. The initials' meanings are as follows:

- *L* stands for *lesbian*, or a woman who is sexually attracted to other women.
- *G* stands for *gay*; this word is sometimes used as a synonym for *homosexual* but often refers to a man who is sexually attracted to other men.
- *B* is *bisexual*, or a person who is sexually attracted to both women and men.
- *T* is *transgender*, or a person whose gender identity does not correspond with the one the person was given at birth.
- *Q* means *queer*, an umbrella term that can refer to anyone in the categories above; it is especially popular among younger people.

signed to overturn Trump's policy, though as of early 2020 it was unclear whether these bills can pass Congress—or survive a potential presidential veto. And a number of transgender troops are suing to have the policy declared unconstitutional. They are backed in these efforts by pro-LGBTQ organizations such as the Human Rights Campaign and the American Civil Liberties Union. Still, the outcome of these lawsuits is uncertain. "I know we are facing an uphill battle," says one transgender soldier. "My goal is to right this wrong."[3]

The treatment of transgender individuals in the military was a particularly difficult outcome for LGBTQ activists. After years of struggle, they had reached their goal of opening the military to transgender people—only to see the policy changed and the prize taken away. In another sense, though, the policy change was nothing new. The story of LGBTQ activism is the story of small victories and incremental changes, often in the face of enormous opposition. The ban on transgender troops was not the first defeat the movement has suffered, and it likely will not be the last.

Tenacity and Resilience

But LGBTQ activism has been an essential part of the story of America during the past half century. As late as the 1960s, homosexual individuals were an almost invisible minority. "America didn't even know gay people,"[4] says LGBTQ activist Mara Keisling. To the extent they were known, they were scorned and avoided. The notion that someday openly gay couples would be allowed to marry; the concept that openly gay people would serve in Congress, fight in the military, and be icons in the entertainment world; the idea that LGBTQ individuals would live lives not much different from their heterosexual counterparts—all of these would have been almost inconceivable to people in the 1960s. That these changes all have come to pass is a testament to the tenacity, passion, and resilience of advocates for LGBTQ rights.

> "America didn't even know gay people."[4]
>
> —LGBTQ activist Mara Keisling

7

Chapter One

Toward Tolerance

Like most of the rest of the world, the United States before the 1960s was not at all friendly to gay people. Being gay was considered a psychological disorder. According to the influential American Psychiatric Association (APA), homosexuality was abnormal and represented a danger to the community. Politicians, police officers, and physicians alike argued that homosexuals—especially male homosexuals—were deviants with one goal: corrupting America's youth by turning young people gay. "Each year thousands of youngsters of high school and college age," warned one newspaper, "are introduced to these unnatural practices by inveterate [incurable] seducers."[5] Homosexuals were called moral weaklings, degenerates, and worse, and society did what it could to contain the menace.

One obvious way of controlling homosexuality was through the use of laws, and governments of the time passed plenty of laws designed to limit the rights of LGBTQ Americans. Same-sex marriage was illegal everywhere; by law, marriage licenses were issued only to couples consisting of one man and one woman. Parents known to be homosexual often lost custody of their children. Government jobs, including the military, were off limits to gay men and lesbians as well. Schools were typically forbidden to hire LGBTQ teachers; if it came out that a faculty or staff member was gay, he or she could expect to be fired on the spot. In Florida alone, about one hundred teachers were fired for being gay from 1957 to 1963.

Public opinion was solidly against lesbians and gay men as well. Few citizens were prepared to speak up for their gay neighbors. Like the politicians who made the laws, ordinary Americans viewed homosexuality with great distaste and wanted to limit its reach. Thus, even when no law prevented private employers from hiring gay men and women, many employers refused to do so; coworkers, customers, or clients might balk at being around a person who was gay. In the same way, landlords frequently refused to rent apartments to gay and lesbian individuals or even to those who they suspected might be homosexual. Parents forced their homosexual children out of their homes or committed them to mental hospitals. No decent person, it seemed, wanted to show sympathy for lesbians and gay men.

Many gay and lesbian people could pass for heterosexual in their daily lives, and given the risks of being open about their sexuality, many of them did exactly that. Some remained single, while others married partners of the opposite sex, trying—often unsuccessfully—to ignore or cover up their sexuality. Still

There was a time in the United States when people who were gay or lesbian were blatantly discriminated against and public opinion was strongly anti-homosexuality.

"All I wanted was to be straight so my parents could be happy. They never, never knew."[6]

—Author and illustrator Maurice Sendak

others had longtime same-sex partners whom they spoke of simply as roommates or friends. Author and illustrator Maurice Sendak, for example, had a fifty-year relationship with a man but refused to tell his parents. "All I wanted was to be straight so my parents could be happy," he told an interviewer years later. "They never, never knew."[6]

Gay Bars

There were, however, several ways in which LGBTQ Americans could connect with one another during this time. One of these was by gathering in gay bars—drinking establishments catering to LGBTQ individuals. Even before the 1960s, gay bars were operating in large US cities. Lesbians and gay men could meet each other in these bars to socialize, drink, and sometimes dance in an atmosphere where hiding their sexuality was unnecessary. "Saturday night is the gayest night of the week," a reporter wrote in 1962 about the popularity of gay bars in Philadelphia. The bars, the article noted, were frequented by a variety of patrons: "Handsome young men in natty, continental-style suits, rough-hewn workers in khaki pants and jackets, [and] aging, pot-bellied executives in conservative business suits."[7]

Still, these places were in no sense a safe space for customers. Engaging in activities such as dancing with a person of the same sex was often against the law. So was dressing as a member of the opposite sex, which was popular among some male patrons of the bars and a few females as well. "I have been arrested in New York more times than I have fingers and toes for wearing pants and a shirt,"[8] complained one woman who liked wearing men's clothing. Many gay bars lacked proper liquor licenses, moreover, and some turned a blind eye to drug deals taking place on the property.

Gay bars thus typically operated on the fringes of the law, and so police frequently staged raids on these businesses. That presented several issues for patrons. Most notably, customers ran the risk of being arrested—often for no crime greater than wearing a skirt or kissing a person of the same gender. Even if customers were not charged with a crime, moreover, it was possible that a zealous journalist covering the raid might reveal their identities. And the police often treated customers of gay bars with unnecessary roughness, both verbally and physically. Still, there seemed little that patrons could do when police arrived except to follow directions and hope to avoid any trouble.

The Mattachine Society and the Daughters of Bilitis

Beginning in the 1950s, a few organizations sprang up to fight for the rights of LGBTQ Americans. The Mattachine Society, formed in 1950, was among the first of these groups. The organization was designed in part to help gay men who were facing discrimination and oppression in their lives. The Daughters of Bilitis, a similar group focused on lesbians, formed in 1955. Though the leaders of these groups were often open about their sexuality, rank-and-file members generally were not. The Daughters of Bilitis, for example, guaranteed anonymity to any member who did not wish to make her sexuality known to the general public.

At first, these groups kept a low profile. Their primary focus was supporting the gay community in relatively small yet important ways. They provided safe spaces, for example, where gay people could meet and talk. They offered legal advice to men and women who had run afoul of antigay laws. They also worked to educate gay and lesbian people about issues related to sexuality. For example, their newsletters contained arguments from medical professionals who believed that homosexuality was not a disorder. For the most part, though, these organizations were not confrontational. In particular, they rarely engaged in direct political action. Gay leaders of the 1950s and early 1960s typically believed that holding marches or rallies would do more to alienate the general public than it would to further their cause.

Stonewall

That changed, however, in the early morning hours of June 28, 1969. One of the most popular gay bars in the country was the Stonewall Inn, which was located in the Greenwich Village section of Manhattan. The Stonewall Inn was regularly raided by police officers. But when New York City police entered the bar soon after 1:00 a.m. on the 28th, patrons fought back. Instead of disappearing into the night when they were allowed to leave the bar, they gathered on the sidewalk outside the bar and heckled the officers. Many refused to produce identification; others fought back against police. People in the neighborhood, realizing what was happening, came to the bar to show support for the customers. "Everyone's restless, angry and high-spirited," recalls a man who had been walking near the bar. "Something's brewing."[9]

    The situation soon deteriorated. Rumors spread through the crowd that people inside the building were being beaten. At one point a woman came out of the bar in handcuffs and challenged the crowd. "Why don't you guys do something?"[10] she demand-

The Stonewall rebellion marked a turning point in the gay liberation movement. It was named after the famed Stonewall Inn gay bar (pictured), which is located in New York City's Greenwich Village.

ed. The crowd responded by throwing beer bottles, smashing windows, and attacking police officers—some of whom sought safety by barricading themselves inside the bar. Within a few hours order had been restored at the scene, but sporadic riots continued over the next few days.

The Stonewall rebellion marked a turning point in the gay liberation movement. For the first time, gay men and lesbians fought back against the injustices they suffered on a regular basis. Instead of living out of the limelight, LGBTQ Americans realized that they could emulate African Americans, Hispanics, and women, all of whom had coalesced earlier to form liberation movements. Just as these groups had demanded tolerance of who they were from more powerful majorities, now LGBTQ Americans felt empowered to do the same. "Gay power! Isn't that great?" said poet Allen Ginsberg, a gay man, when he heard about the rebellion. "It's about time we did something to assert ourselves."[11]

> "Gay power! Isn't that great? It's about time we did something to assert ourselves."[11]
>
> —Gay poet Allen Ginsberg

Gay Visibility

During the early 1970s, the trend toward increased tolerance and visibility continued. Because the APA classified homosexuality as a mental illness, lesbians or gay men who sought psychiatric help for any reason could expect to have many if not all of their problems blamed on their sexuality. Indeed, it was common for mental health practitioners to try to "cure" homosexuals by converting them to heterosexuality. In the early 1970s, though, LGBTQ activists lobbied the APA to remove homosexuality from its list of mental disorders, and in 1973 the organization did exactly that. As an APA resolution put it, "We will no longer insist on a label of sickness for individuals who insist that they are well and demonstrate no generalized impairment in social effectiveness."[12]

In fact, the APA's resolution did not simply redefine homosexuality in medical terms. It also spoke out on the wider question of discrimination based on sexual orientation, strongly recommending

The Gay Liberation Front

The Gay Liberation Front (GLF) was a radical organization formed soon after the Stonewall rebellion. The GLF supported not only gay rights but various other political struggles, such as the fight against racism. It also attacked traditional gender roles. Karla Jay, a New York resident in 1969, recalled an early meeting of the GLF and contrasted the ideals of the time with more recent experiences.

> It's really amazing what has happened. In the early summer of 1969, after the Stonewall uprising, we had the first Gay Liberation Front meetings. We sat in a circle, and we went around and asked each other what we wanted from liberation. One woman said, "I would like to be able to hold my lover's hand in public and not be beaten up." And we all could agree to that. Another woman said, "I would like to get married." We laughed, and we thought, someone should get a straightjacket for this woman because she's living in fantasyland.
>
> To have seen the progress that we have made in the LGBT community, here we have things like marriage, where so many couples—and non-couples too—have children, and where so many employers accept us and give us benefits. These things are really quite extraordinary.

Quoted in Joshua Barajas and Gretchen Frazee, "What Stonewall Means to the People Who Were There," PBS.org, June 26, 2019. www.pbs.org.

that governments recognize that gay and lesbian people were entitled to civil rights—the natural rights that people have by being part of a society. "[The APA] supports and urges the enactment of civil rights legislation at local, state, and Federal levels that would insure homosexual citizens the same protections now guaranteed to others," the resolution read. At the same time, APA leaders called on states to change the way they treated homosexual behavior. Recognizing that nearly all states at the time criminalized homosexual activity, the resolution advocated "the repeal of all legislation making criminal offense of sexual acts performed by consenting adults in private."[13]

Most gay rights leaders were delighted by the APA's change of heart. The National Gay Task Force, based in New York City, described the resolution as "the greatest gay victory" and noted that the APA's actions had the effect of removing "the cornerstone of oppression"[14] for lesbians and gay men. In part emboldened by the APA resolution, openly gay men and women began to move more and more rapidly into the mainstream of American life. In 1974, for example, a gay woman named Kathy Kozachenko was elected to a seat on the city council of Ann Arbor, Michigan, becoming the first openly gay person to win a vote for public office in America. Later that year, Elaine Noble became the first to serve in statewide office when she was elected to the Massachusetts legislature. Others followed, including Harvey Milk, elected a city supervisor of San Francisco in 1977—and tragically killed, along with San Francisco mayor George Moscone, the following year.

Visibility increased in other areas as well. Lesbians and gay men became more and more open about their sexuality on college campuses. In 1968 there were no gay and lesbian student centers and no school-funded gay student groups at any American college. By

In the 1970s gay and lesbian college students started being more open about their sexuality. By 1975 hundreds of gay and lesbian student centers and school-funded gay student groups were operating at American colleges.

"This coming out of gay groups is one of the most positive things to happen on this campus."[15]

—Dean Paul Ginsberg, University of Wisconsin

1975 there were hundreds. "This coming out of gay groups is one of the most positive things to happen on this campus,"[15] noted Paul Ginsberg, the dean of students at the University of Wisconsin in 1974. Homosexuality likewise began moving into the mainstream in entertainment. In 1977, for example, actor Billy Crystal portrayed a gay man in a prime-time television show called *Soap*.

Disappointments

The gains during this period were not consistent, however. In 1975 New York representative Bella Abzug introduced a bill in the US House of Representatives that would have prohibited discrimination because of sexual preference in many areas of American life. The bill never was taken up for a vote. That same year US Air Force officer Leonard Matlovich told his commanding officer that he was gay. Despite having been recognized for heroism in the Vietnam War, Matlovich was forced to leave the military. And while many colleges were accepting of the movement toward gay student organizations, others, such as Penn State University and the University of Kansas, tried to block these organizations from forming or at least from doing so with university funds.

In some cases pushback from antigay activists succeeded in rolling back gains by the gay rights movement. This was perhaps most notable in 1977, when Dade County, Florida, passed an ordinance banning discrimination against gay men and lesbians in jobs, housing, and other areas. The ordinance was greeted enthusiastically by gay people in Dade County and beyond. But it was bitterly opposed by many others. Opponents of the ordinance asserted that homosexuality was sinful and perverted, and they argued that the children of the community would be in danger if the ordinance was allowed to stand. "I would not want a known homosexual teaching my children,"[16] said Florida's governor, Reubin Askew.

In Florida, as in many other states, unpopular new ordinances can be overturned by a direct vote of citizens. Getting the measure on the ballot required the signatures of ten thousand voters; in a warning sign for the gay rights movement, opponents gathered six times that number. Led by a celebrity named Anita Bryant, who had been a singer, beauty queen, and spokesperson for the Florida orange juice industry, the anti-ordinance forces were ultimately successful: the people of Dade County repealed the ordinance by a margin of greater than two to one. For those who supported gay rights, the result was devastating. Ruth Shack, the politician who first proposed the ordinance, described the outcome as "three times worse than I ever expected. . . . It was a huge step back."[17]

> "I would not want a known homosexual teaching my children."[16]
>
> —Former Florida governor Reubin Askew

The effects of the vote were felt far beyond Dade County. Many other American communities had passed similar antidiscrimination ordinances, but following the repeal of the ordinance in Dade County, these likewise came under attack. Bryant traveled around the country encouraging voters to reject these ordinances, often tailoring her message to conservative Christians; gay activists, she charged, were fighting a "disguised attack on God."[18] The rhetoric was often effective. In several cities, such as Eugene, Oregon, voters overturned antidiscrimination ordinances, just as their counterparts had done in Dade County.

Optimism

However, the news for gay activists was not all bad. In late 1977 Seattle, Washington, held a referendum in which citizens voted to uphold their city's new antidiscrimination ordinance. The following year voters soundly rejected an initiative on the ballot in California that would have prohibited gay and lesbian people from working in the state's school systems. Gay activists fought back in other ways as well. Bryant's ties to the orange juice industry in Florida led gay leaders to start a national campaign to boycott Florida orange juice. When a television production company announced plans to have Bryant star in a show, angry activists convinced the company to rescind its offer.

By the end of the 1970s, gay and lesbian activists knew they still had a long way to go. In much of the country, discrimination against LGBTQ people was legal—and frequent. Large numbers of gay men and lesbians still felt a need to hide their sexuality. Still, the world had changed considerably since the Stonewall raid in 1969. Gay rights activists had raised Americans' tolerance of lesbians and gay men, chipped away at the degree to which homosexuality was hated and feared, and worked successfully to win at least some legal protections for homosexual people. By any standard, the gay rights movement was making enormous headway.

Chapter Two

The AIDS Crisis

The progress of the 1970s was dramatic. However, it was also short lived. In the early 1980s a disease called AIDS, or acquired immune deficiency syndrome, began to appear in the United States. Though AIDS could—and did—infect anyone, it was primarily transmitted through sexual contact and was especially prevalent at that time among gay men. AIDS is a horrifying condition that severely weakens the immune system of those who have it. It causes intense suffering in patients, typically over a period of months or years, and in the 1980s at least, all those who contracted AIDS died from it. "AIDS was a death sentence," journalist Trevor Martin writes, recalling a time when Martin's friend Steve revealed to him that he was infected. "Steve was telling me he was going to die."[19]

AIDS was devastating to the gay community. In part that was because of the enormous death toll; by the early 1990s AIDS was killing more than twenty thousand Americans each year, many of them gay men. But the AIDS epidemic had a negative impact on the LGBTQ community in another way as well. The connection between homosexuality and AIDS alarmed millions of Americans. Though the disease could not be caught through casual contact with an infected person, many people responded with fear and anger. They avoided interactions with gay men and lobbied in some cases for severe measures aimed at the gay community in an effort to ensure that the disease did not spread further. If the 1970s

In this 1989 photo, an AIDS patient is comforted by his partner. AIDS is a horrible, painful disease, and during the 1980s no one who got AIDS survived.

had been a time of increased tolerance for gay people, the 1980s and early 1990s represented the opposite.

During this era, the LGBTQ community was forced to spend much of its time and energy helping the victims of the disease. But despite the practical demands of caring for AIDS patients during an epidemic, the fight for gay rights did not come to an end. Indeed, the need for activism was in some ways greater than ever. Landlords were evicting gay men from apartments; doctors were refusing to treat people they thought might be infected; government leaders were demonizing those who had the disease. With the gay community in crisis, new activist groups sprang up to push back against those who would further erode the rights of LGBTQ Americans. Successful in many ways yet frustratingly unsuccessful in others, the activism of the AIDS era stands out as a remarkable period in the struggle for gay rights.

HIV and AIDS

In the early 1980s, doctors in several large American cities noticed a perplexing pattern. Some of their patients were developing uncommon yet deadly illnesses, notably a lung infection known as PCP and a cancer called Kaposi's sarcoma. More curious still, the new patients did not fit the usual profile of people who were likely to contract these conditions. Although Kaposi's sarcoma, for example, tended to affect older men, most of the new patients with the illness were much younger. Physicians recognized that the diseases were caused by some underlying problem with the patients' immune system, but were initially at a loss to explain it.

Before long, however, the situation became clearer. Caused by the human immunodeficiency virus (HIV), AIDS is a condition that drastically weakens the immune system and makes the body vulnerable to all kinds of infections. Doctors soon learned that AIDS was transmitted through body fluids such as blood and semen. Still, many people during the early 1980s feared that AIDS could also be spread by casual contact—that is, by skin-to-skin transmission or by breathing the same air, much like influenza or the common cold. Thus, Americans of the period worried that they could contract the virus simply by shaking the hand of an infected person or perhaps even by shopping in the same store as someone with the disease.

The fear of catching AIDS, coupled with the common belief of the time that homosexuality was unnatural and immoral, led many Americans to develop a deep hostility toward AIDS patients. Many of these people contended that the gay men who contracted AIDS were simply getting what they deserved. Politician and speechwriter Patrick Buchanan, for example, wrote in 1984 that gay men "had declared war upon nature, and now nature is exacting an awful retribution."[20] Government leaders and ordinary people alike—often ignoring the science about AIDS transmission and still believing that casual contact could spread HIV—debated what

> "[Gay men] had declared war upon nature, and now nature is exacting an awful retribution."[20]
>
> —Politician and speechwriter Patrick Buchanan

measures should be taken to safeguard the rest of the population from those who had AIDS. More often than not, these measures paid little or no attention to the feelings or needs of AIDS patients: the point in most cases was to separate the sick for the benefit of the healthy.

The result was a series of discriminatory actions taken against those with the disease—a group consisting largely, though not entirely, of gay men. Landlords refused to rent apartments to openly gay men for fear that the men would infect others in the building. Employers fired workers who they believed might have AIDS. Some suggested that people with AIDS should be barred from working in food services or health care, lest they infect customers or patients. Ryan White, an Indiana teenager who contracted AIDS through tainted blood products, was barred from attending middle school in 1985; a year later a Massachusetts lawyer named Geoffrey Bowers was fired from his law firm after contracting the illness.

> "We were terrorized. We'd see 25-year-old handsome young men waste down to where they looked 95."[21]
>
> —LGBTQ activist Kenneth Bunch

For gay men of the 1980s, then, AIDS represented a double blow. First and most important, thousands of them were dying long, drawn-out deaths. "We were terrorized," says activist Kenneth Bunch. "We'd see 25-year-old handsome young men waste down to where they looked 95."[21] In addition to knowing they would soon die, moreover, patients with AIDS also knew that they were viewed with suspicion, fear, and even hatred by a substantial number of their fellow Americans. For these reasons, much of the focus of gay activism in the 1980s was on AIDS. Advocates for AIDS patients pushed for more research into the disease, did their best to make people with AIDS comfortable in their final months, and fought discrimination as best they could.

Support for Gay Men

One of the first organizations set up to lobby for gay men in the AIDS era was called the Gay Men's Health Crisis (GMHC). Founded in New York City by several gay men in early 1982, the GMHC

AIDS in 1981

Alvin Friedman-Kien was a physician who saw some of the first cases of AIDS in New York City. Years later he recalled one of his first patients in this excerpt from a longer interview:

> He had enlarged lymph nodes, he had fever, weight loss, large spleen; and incidentally he had some brownish purple spots on his lower extremities which were ignored by all the physicians who were taking care of him. They removed his spleen, did lymph node biopsies and liver biopsies with no finalized diagnosis. And he was discharged: but he said to me, when he finally came to see me, "nobody would look at my feet, at the rash on my feet." They were faint, they were purple-lavender, they looked like bruises. In any case, I did a biopsy and quite surprisingly it came back as Kaposi's sarcoma. . . . It didn't look typical, because prior to that man I had only seen maybe seven or eight cases of classical Kaposi's sarcoma, usually in elderly men of Eastern European or Mediterranean origins. . . . They had purple sores on the lower extremities and the longevity was 10 to 15 years. . . . But then, not two weeks later, I saw another man, an actor, who was perfectly healthy and he just had pink-purple spots on his face, and he couldn't cover them up with makeup anymore.

Quoted in Ronald Bayer and Gerald M. Oppenheimer, *AIDS Doctors: Voices from the Epidemic: An Oral History.* New York: Oxford University, 2000, pp. 13–14.

began as a small organization. Larry Kramer, one of its founders, describes it as a "struggling ragtag group of really frightened and mostly young men."[22] The GMHC quickly filled a need in New York's gay community. It offered legal help to AIDS patients who were facing discrimination. It also provided crisis counseling and practical help, such as assistance in finding a job or a place to live. And it taught sexually active people to use condoms in order to avoid the risk of AIDS. (Condoms block the transmission of semen, thus preventing the disease from spreading.)

The GMHC was in most ways a highly successful organization. Its ability to raise funds for AIDS research and AIDS patients was particularly impressive. In early 1983, for example, the GMHC sponsored a fund-raising event at New York City's Madison Square Garden. Organizers bought all the tickets for a performance of the Ringling Brothers and Barnum & Bailey Circus in advance and sold them to people who supported their cause. The event attracted a full house and earned the GMHC $250,000. Two years later the GMHC sponsored an art auction that raised over $1 million. The money helped the organization hire more staff and provide more services.

The GMHC was also involved more directly in political activism. It was most notable for its work on AIDS discrimination suits, in which AIDS patients sued employers or landlords who denied them their basic rights. In 1983 GMHC funds largely underwrote the costs of the first of these lawsuits. However, for some members the GMHC was not political enough. Kramer, in particular, believed that the organization needed to fight harder, even at the risk of becoming more controversial. Many board members disagreed. "They didn't like [it] when I would raise my voice," Kramer remembers, "when I would criticize the mayor [of New York City]."[23]

Recognizing that he could not pull the GMHC in a more activist direction, Kramer decided to leave the group. In March 1987 he gave a speech in which he asked the audience, "Do we want to start a new organization devoted to political action?" One observer reports that Kramer's listeners responded with "a resounding yes."[24] Within days Kramer and others had founded a new and specifically political organization. The group was officially called the AIDS Coalition to Unleash Power, but most people knew it by its initials: ACT UP.

ACT UP

From the beginning ACT UP focused on political activism. Shortly after the group was formed, 250 members of the group staged a demonstration in New York City. The protesters demanded that the federal government establish a national policy to fight AIDS.

They also wanted AIDS patients to be allowed access to experimental drugs not yet approved for use. "We are angry, we want action!"[25] protesters shouted. When police ordered the protesters to disperse, many refused, and seventeen people were arrested and charged with civil disobedience.

The arrests did not come as a shock to ACT UP's leaders; in fact, they hoped to have some protesters taken into custody. ACT UP members believed that the arrests would attract the attention of the media and allow the group to share their grievances

Hundreds of members of the AIDS activist group ACT UP participate in a 1992 die-in protest in Washington, DC. The group was founded by activist Larry Kramer, who believed that collective outrage was the only way to save the gay community from the AIDS epidemic.

with a wider audience, thus bringing pressure to bear on powerful people and organizations. Indeed, the US Food and Drug Administration announced soon after the protest that it would shorten the drug approval process, making experimental drugs available to the public earlier than before. Many observers attributed the change in policy to the protest.

Kramer and ACT UP were only getting started. Kramer firmly believed that only outrage could save the gay community from the AIDS epidemic. Without confrontation, Kramer argued, government officials would never do anything to help AIDS patients or end the discrimination they experienced. "Our continued existence," he once said, referring to gay men as a group, "depends on just how angry you can get."[26] In 1988 ACT UP repeated its demonstration in the streets of New York City; this time one hundred activists were arrested. The following year, seven ACT UP members chained themselves to a balcony at the New York Stock Exchange to protest the high cost of the AIDS drug AZT. Though

ACT UP and Stonewall

In this excerpt from a longer article, documentary filmmaker Jim Hubbard describes the differences and similarities between the ACT UP movement of the 1980s and 1990s and the Stonewall rebellion of 1969.

ACT UP . . . was the first great leap for the queer movement after Stonewall. . . . ACT UP brought real power to queer people for the first time. The events and subsequent grassroots political action that we now refer to as Stonewall brought visibility and self-esteem. Stonewall may have been more important for the changes it brought to the community than to the changes it made to the larger society. ACT UP, in contrast, changed the whole country. For the first time, the general public saw queer people as determined, strong, smart, articulate, and having a modicum of power.

Jim Hubbard, "ACT UP Changed Everything," *The Nation*, June 29, 2019. www.thenation.com.

a year's supply of the drug cost thousands of dollars and insurance companies typically did not cover its cost, AZT was at the time the only drug known to slow the progress of AIDS.

Over the next few years, ACT UP took part in even more protests, some of which caused great controversy. One of the group's targets was the Roman Catholic Church. The church held that sex should be reserved for only heterosexual married couples. Homosexuality, in the eyes of the church, was a sin; so was sex outside of marriage. So, too, was any kind of artificial birth control. Accordingly, the church attempted to block efforts on the part of activists to distribute condoms or advocate their use in New York City high schools. In 1989 ACT UP members staged a demonstration during a service in New York's St. Patrick's Cathedral. The protest was chaotic, with protesters screaming during the sermon, chaining themselves to pews, and throwing condoms to disrupt the proceedings. Though Kramer felt that the demonstration had been a big success, others worried that the event may have done the activists more harm than good.

> "Our continued existence [as a gay community] depends on just how angry you can get."[26]
>
> —ACT UP founder Larry Kramer

Government and AIDS

Still, there seemed little question that ACT UP's overall strategy was working. In the first years of the crisis, the government had been slow to respond to the situation. Money for medical research was lacking, help for AIDS patients was minimal, and some government officials seemed determined to ignore AIDS as much as possible. Ronald Reagan's first term as US president began in 1981, just as AIDS was starting to spread, but Reagan paid little attention to the disease. "The Reagan administration's first reaction was chilling," one reporter writes, noting that presidential spokesperson Larry Speakes had seemed to mock AIDS patients in a 1984 press conference. The administration, the reporter added "appeared to treat the epidemic as a joke."[27] Indeed, Reagan did not even mention AIDS in a speech until 1987, less than two years before he left office.

In the late 1980s and early 1990s, though, the government's attitude began to change. In 1990, for instance, Congress passed the Americans with Disabilities Act (ADA). Among other provisions, this law made it illegal to discriminate against the disabled. AIDS qualified as a disability when the act was passed; thus, discrimination against AIDS patients became against the law. Funding for AIDS research and programs rose sharply in the second half of the 1980s, and the federal government began running public service announcements and sending out mass mailings to educate Americans about AIDS.

Ronald Reagan, the fortieth president of the United States, paid little attention to the onset and spread of AIDS. He made no mention of the disease in any of his speeches until 1987, when he had been in office for six years.

The work of advocacy organizations like the GMHC and ACT UP played a major role in bringing about these changes. Their tireless support for AIDS patients helped convince other Americans that people with AIDS deserved sympathy and practical help, not scorn and fear. Their steady attacks on discrimination helped other Americans realize that preventing people with AIDS from finding housing and jobs was neither useful nor just. Their protests against antiquated rules regarding drug approval pushed the government to amend its policies. And the dramatic techniques used by groups such as ACT UP guaranteed that Americans would pay attention to the issues raised by AIDS.

In the mid-1990s drugs were developed that could keep AIDS patients alive—and in reasonable health—for years. "Doctors are starting to consider HIV a chronic, manageable disease rather than a death sentence,"[28] *Newsweek* magazine reported in December 1996 in a story titled "The End of AIDS?" The decades since have proved this new perspective largely accurate. To be sure, not all American AIDS patients receive the drugs for various reasons. And AIDS remains a leading cause of sickness and death in parts of the developing world. But AIDS is no longer the plague it was in the 1980s and early 1990s, when virtually everyone with the disease died from it. And for that, Americans have the activists of the 1980s to thank.

Chapter Three

The Struggle for Acceptance

Following the dark days of the AIDS crisis, LGBTQ activism took on a new and different character. Beginning in the 1990s LGBTQ advocates focused on two paths in order to win their rights. The first path involved the legal system. Most of the great strides taken by the LGBTQ movement during the 1990s and the early twenty-first century were the result of court cases. The overarching strategy was to identify an injustice or inequity, bring a lawsuit alleging that the discrimination was not in keeping with the Constitution, and then marshal arguments strong enough to sway the opinions of the judges who would decide the case. This strategy was highly effective. Similarly, gay and lesbian people were sometimes able to persuade legislators to act directly on their behalf by passing new laws, though this could be more difficult.

The other prong of LGBTQ advocacy during this time involved public opinion. Earlier activists had fought for tolerance. Stonewall was in some sense a rebellion against the invisibility of lesbians and gay men. The activists of the time did not especially care how they were viewed by the heterosexual majority; they cared much more about being left alone to live their lives as they pleased without fear of imprisonment. After the AIDS crisis, the focus on tolerance gave way to a focus on acceptance. LGBTQ Americans increasingly demanded to be seen as full and equal members of society, just like any heterosexual American. Much of gay and lesbian activism from the 1990s through the mid-2010s focused on changing the law or on changing the way people thought about sexuality.

Don't Ask, Don't Tell

One of the first areas addressed by activists of this period involved the military. Gay men and lesbians had served in the armed forces of the United States for years but never openly. Indeed, a member of the military who announced his or her homosexuality—or who was found in a sexual situation with a same-sex partner—could expect to be forced out of the service immediately, often with a dishonorable discharge. That also applied to personnel whose peers or superiors merely suspected that they were gay. The official policy of the government, as expressed by the US Department of Defense in 1982, was that "homosexuality is incompatible with military service."[29]

In the early 1990s this became an intolerable situation for many gay men and women who were serving in the military, as well as for others who wanted to serve. They were no longer willing to hide their sexuality in order to continue the work they were doing and no longer saw any reason why they could not be open about their lives. In 1992, thanks in part to pressure from LGBTQ activists, all the Democratic candidates for president promised that if elected, they would try to allow gay and lesbian people to serve. Indeed, Democrat Bill Clinton was elected president that year, and early in his term he did set out to overturn the existing policy.

Clinton was only partially successful. Many politicians and military leaders bitterly opposed any attempt to allow lesbians and gay men to serve in the armed forces. Their main concern was that heterosexual troops would object and therefore that the presence of gay people would lower morale. In the end the two

> "Homosexuality is incompatible with military service."[29]
>
> —US Department of Defense in 1982

From the 1990s through the mid-2010s, a major focus for gay and lesbian activists was on changing discriminatory laws. One of the first areas addressed involved the military, since gay men and lesbians could be forced out of service if they were open about their sexuality.

sides reached a compromise. They agreed that gay people had the same right to serve as heterosexual people and that officers could not ask military personnel about their sexuality. At the same time, however, the compromise specified that homosexual individuals in the military were not allowed to identify themselves as gay. If they did, they still would be subject to removal from the armed forces. This policy quickly became known as Don't Ask, Don't Tell, or DADT.

DADT was controversial from the start. Even Clinton admitted that the policy was "not a perfect solution." Nevertheless, he argued that the policy represented a "major step forward,"[30] and many LGBTQ activists agreed. According to this view, Clinton had gotten the best deal that gay and lesbian people could have hoped for. But other activists were displeased. They believed that the new policy was too similar to the old and that it did little or nothing to ensure acceptance of gay people among the military ranks. Despite the intense opposition to change, they argued, Clinton could—and should—have gotten a better deal.

In the years following its implementation, DADT grew steadily less popular. The ban on openness in the military increasingly rankled activists—and increasingly bothered many politicians, especially in the Democratic Party. At the same time, surveys showed that a growing number of military personnel supported repeal of DADT and that this opinion was shared among the general public as well. During his 2008 campaign for president, Barack Obama pledged to repeal DADT, and in 2010 he signed a bill that did exactly that. Today DADT is not remembered fondly by many LGBTQ activists, and for good reason; but at the time, it did represent a significant change in how gay people were perceived in America.

Lawrence v. Texas

Another victory for gay rights came in 2003 with a court case called *Lawrence v. Texas*. In 1998 Texas residents John Lawrence and Tyron Garner were arrested for sodomy—that is, engaging in anal or oral sex. Sodomy had been a crime in most states for years. As of 1960, in fact, every US state banned it. While people were seldom arrested for sodomy, the laws were there for any zealous prosecutor to use as a weapon against the gay community. As the gay rights movement gathered steam, most states began repealing their anti-sodomy laws. But by 1998 fourteen states still banned sodomy. Among them was Texas.

Lawrence and Garner were convicted and forced to pay a fine. But they fought back. With the assistance of a gay rights organization called Lambda Legal, the two men sought to overturn Texas's anti-sodomy law. The men argued that the Constitution protected a right to privacy, a right largely established by courts during the 1960s and 1970s. Since Lawrence and Garner had been engaged in consensual sex in Lawrence's home, the men asserted, the government had no business regulating their sex lives. They also pointed out that in Texas, a man and a woman could legally engage in sodomy, but two men could not. This, they argued, was discriminatory treatment that violated the Constitution.

The case made its way slowly through the legal system until it reached the Supreme Court in 2003. There, the justices ruled 6–3 that the men had been wrongly arrested. As Justice Anthony Kennedy wrote for the majority, "The petitioners [Lawrence and Garner] are entitled to respect for their private lives. The State cannot demean their existence or control their destiny by making their private sexual conduct a crime."[31] The decision overturned the anti-sodomy law not only in Texas but in the other states that still had these laws as well. Consensual sex was now legal for gay men throughout the country.

Adoption

Family life was another major area of concern for gay activists during this time. One particularly complex topic involved adoption. LGBTQ couples, like heterosexual couples, often want to adopt children. For years, though, the laws in many states prohibited adoption by people who were openly gay, whether single or part of a gay couple. The reason for this ban rested on the notion that children were meant to have a male parent and a female parent, and that gay and lesbian parents were unfit to raise children. As former Florida governor Jeb Bush put it in 2005, "It is in the best interest of adoptive children . . . to be placed in a home anchored both by a father and a mother."[32]

Advocates for LGBTQ adoption rejected Bush's perspective. Research, they pointed out, overwhelmingly showed that children raised by gay parents turned out as well adjusted as children raised by heterosexual parents. They also noted that there were more children needing homes than there were heterosexual people interesting in adopting them, especially among older children. Refusing to allow gay people to adopt often meant consigning children to years in foster care rather than placing them in loving homes. Finally, the advocates argued that LGBTQ people

Federalism

The United States has a federal system of government. Under this system, some powers are given to the national, or federal, government. Others are reserved for state and local governments. The founders of the country chose a federal system in part as a compromise, and it has often been an uneasy one. In the years since the ratification of the Constitution in 1789, the tension between the rights of states and the power of the federal government has been a frequent theme in American politics.

The federal system explains some of the inconsistencies in the rights enjoyed by LGBTQ people in different parts of the country. For some aspects of life, such as the military, federal laws and rules prevail; states have essentially no say over who participates in the nation's armed forces. However, states generally have the authority to pass laws regulating the conduct of their citizens. That explains why same-sex marriage was legal in some states but not others. There is one standard that pertains to all laws, however. This is the standard set by the US Constitution. In the *Obergefell* and *Lawrence* cases, the US Supreme Court determined that the laws of individual states conflicted with the Constitution. Thus, all such laws were deemed unconstitutional.

could indeed be excellent parents. "My partner and I have been together for 11 years," one gay man told Bush. "We have a lot to offer a child, love, the finest schools, and good moral standing."[33]

Little by little, the forces for gay adoption began to carry the day. Part of the reason involved shifting public opinion. In 1994 a poll revealed that only 28 percent of Americans thought that gay and lesbian people should have the right to adopt children. In 1999 a similar survey revealed that this percentage had risen a few points. By 2008 about 40 percent approved of LGBTQ adoption, and in a survey taken in 2012 the approval rate had shot up dramatically to 61 percent. Adoption

> "My partner and I have been together for 11 years. We have a lot to offer a child, love, the finest schools, and good moral standing."[33]
>
> —A gay man in Florida wishing to adopt

by gay and lesbian people was moving rapidly toward the mainstream as LGBTQ individuals gained acceptance by Americans. This change in public opinion led some states to overturn the bans they once had on LGBTQ adoption.

But public opinion was not enough. LGBTQ advocates recognized that many states, especially in the South, would likely continue to prevent gay and lesbian people from adopting children. Accordingly, LGBTQ people in these states began to sue when denied the right to adopt. Most, but not all, of these cases have been decided in favor of the plaintiffs. In Florida, for example, a gay couple who had served as foster parents to two boys sued to be allowed to adopt them. In 2008 a judge ruled that the existing law was in violation of the rights of both the gay couple and of the

Many LGBTQ couples want to adopt children. Although they often can today, it was impossible for years because laws in many states prohibited adoption by individuals or couples who were openly gay.

boys. Though the state appealed, higher courts agreed with the ruling, and the Florida law was officially overturned in 2010.

Still, to eliminate laws one state at a time was inefficient and slow, and activists looked for a case that might establish adoption rights for LGBTQ people throughout the country. That came in 2017. At the time, Arkansas law said that children's birth certificates could not list the names of two same-sex parents—a convoluted way of discouraging adoption by gay couples. Two lesbian couples challenged the law. The US Supreme Court eventually put an end to the controversy by not only striking down the Arkansas law but ruling that LGBTQ couples could henceforth adopt across the United States. "Victory!"[34] exulted GLAD, a legal advocacy group for the LGBTQ community.

Marriage Equality

The struggle to win adoption rights was contentious—but not nearly as contentious as the struggle for marriage equality, or the right of same-sex couples to marry. In some sense the right of LGBTQ people to marry represents the ultimate in their growing acceptance in American culture. Marriage, after all, has been at the heart of family life throughout US history. Defining marriage to include same-sex couples has represented a major shift in the way LGBTQ people are viewed by society.

The path to same-sex marriage was long and complex. The controversy began in earnest during the mid-1990s. Hawaii struck the first blow in 1993, when its Supreme Court ruled that denying same-sex couples the right to marry violated the state's constitution. Alarmed by the possibility that judges elsewhere might do the same, federal lawmakers passed a bill in 1996 called the Defense of Marriage Act, or DOMA. Under this law, the federal government did not view same-sex marriage as legal. Additionally, other states could refuse to recognize same-sex marriages performed in states where such marriages were legal. President Clinton called the law "divisive and unnecessary,"[35] but it had been passed by such a large majority that he signed the bill into law regardless.

The right of same-sex couples to marry has been one of the toughest struggles for gay and lesbian people. Being granted this right is, to some extent, indicative of their growing acceptance in American culture.

For several years following DOMA, the drive for marriage equality had limited success. In 1998 Hawaii voters approved a constitutional amendment banning same-sex marriage, thus overruling the state court's decision. In 2004 two mayors—Jason West of New Paltz, New York, and Gavin Newsom of San Francisco, California—briefly conducted marriage ceremonies for gay and lesbian couples in their communities before being stopped by state officials. A California court ruled same-sex marriage legal for Californians in 2008, only to have voters override the court later that year. In 2009 the Maine legislature approved marriage equality, but voters quickly overturned the new law. Every advancement, it seemed, was followed by a retreat.

But the news for marriage equality was not all bad. In 2003 the Massachusetts Supreme Court ruled that gay and lesbian couples could marry, and this new law was not overturned. Connecticut legalized same-sex marriage in 2008, as did Iowa, New Hampshire, and Vermont a year later, and again these laws remained on the books. And beginning in 2011 the small gains made by the pro–marriage equality movement became a flood. That year the Obama administration announced that it would ignore DOMA, and in 2013 the US Supreme Court declared a key part of DOMA unconstitutional. From 2011 to 2013, too, a dozen states made marriage equality the law, a list that included the high-population states of New York and Illinois.

The *Obergefell* Case

For LGBTQ advocates, though, the best was yet to come. In 2012 several marriage equality cases began to make their way through the federal court system. One of these, *Obergefell v. Kasich*, dealt with a gay couple from Ohio, a state where same-sex marriage was not legal. The men had married in Maryland (where same-sex marriage was legal) and sued Ohio when they discovered that their

A Momentous Decision

The *Obergefell* decision unleashed strong reactions in the LGBTQ community. Those who favored the decision gathered to express their delight with the ruling. In Washington, DC, hundreds of people waved American flags and rainbow flags—a symbol of the gay rights movement—outside the Supreme Court building to show their appreciation for the decision. Many New Yorkers found themselves drawn to the former site of the Stonewall Inn, now once again a gay bar. "I walked in and held back tears," says one woman who visited the site the day the *Obergefell* decision was handed down. "Gay Pride started with a riot. This is the last stand of equality."

Indeed, the impact of the decision reduced many people to tears. One California resident was wearing a US soccer jersey when a reporter spoke to her about the ruling. "Putting the U.S. colors on has so much meaning today," she responded, beginning to cry as she spoke. "It's a great day to be an American and to have equality. . . . To wake up and see all these text messages on my phone and to be told that you are recognized wherever you go in the United States, that's incredible. It really is."

Quoted in Michael Pearson et al., "Here's How America Reacted to Friday's Marriage Equality Ruling," CNN, June 26, 2015. www.cnn.com.

home state would not recognize their marriage. This case was bundled with several other marriage cases from Ohio and neighboring states that did not recognize same-sex marriage. In 2015 the cases were heard by the US Supreme Court under the name *Obergefell v. Hodges*.

The case attracted a great deal of attention. Almost 150 people and organizations submitted what are called amicus curiae briefs—legal opinions from those interested in the outcome of a case. This number remains a record for a Supreme Court case. In the end the court ruled by a 5–4 margin that the Constitution made it illegal for states to refuse to marry same-sex couples and therefore that marriage equality would be the law in every US state. The ruling rested on several legal principles but noted in particular that "marriage is a keystone of our social order." As the decision argued, "There is no difference between same- and opposite-sex couples with respect to this principle."[36] To forbid same-sex couples from marrying, the majority ruled, would be to make gay and lesbian people into second-class citizens.

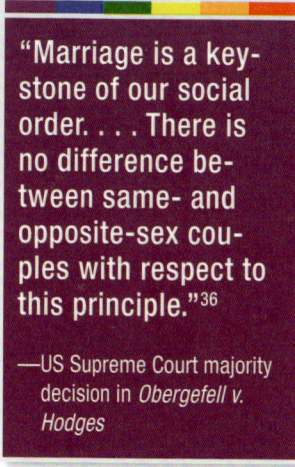

> "Marriage is a keystone of our social order. . . . There is no difference between same- and opposite-sex couples with respect to this principle."[36]
>
> —US Supreme Court majority decision in *Obergefell v. Hodges*

In 1992 LGBTQ Americans had few rights. Battered by the AIDS crisis and marginalized by society, the LGBTQ community was widely shunned and despised. By 2017, though, the status of LGBTQ Americans had changed radically. The right to serve in the military, the right to adopt children, the right to marry: each victory propelled the gay rights movement forward. The use of the legal system and changes in public opinion made these victories possible and led ultimately to an acceptance of gay and lesbian people that would have seemed inconceivable just a quarter century before.

Chapter Four

Transgender Issues

By any standard the status of gay, lesbian, and bisexual Americans has improved dramatically since the time of Stonewall. In most of the country, coming out as gay or bisexual no longer results in the loss of job, home, and family. On the contrary, several million Americans live quite openly as gay men and women. The bulk of Americans support the right of gay and lesbian people to marry and adopt children. Advertisers aim their products at gay audiences. Mainstream movies, books, and television shows include gay men and lesbians as well-rounded, important characters. While prejudice and bias still exist, the gay community enjoys far more rights and acceptance than it did fifty years ago.

That is not the case, however, for transgender Americans. People who are transgender—those who do not identify with the gender they were assigned at birth—not only have experienced significant prejudice, discrimination, and even hatred in the past but continue to do so in the present. The facts are stark. "Significant evidence suggests that transgender persons are often especially . . . vulnerable to harassment and persecution,"[37] reads a judicial opinion in a 2015 court case. Studies indicate that transgender adolescents attempt suicide at a rate up to three times higher than the general teenage population. And transgender people are at least twice as likely to be murdered than people who are not transgender.

Transgender Americans suffer in other ways too. According to the advocacy group National Center for Transgender Equality, about a quarter of transgender Americans have lost jobs on account of their transgender status. Many of the rest have experienced discrimination at work. Lack of money is an issue as well. Transgender individuals are about twice as likely to be homeless as members of the general population—and up to four times as likely to live in extreme poverty. Finally, transgender people often suffer from poor health. AIDS, for example, is more prevalent among transgender Americans than among almost any other group.

In light of these challenges, advocacy for transgender people has been growing. It has taken several forms. One emphasis is on increasing awareness, with transgender people discussing the challenges of being transgender in an often-hostile world. Advocacy can also take a more overtly political approach, with activists staging demonstrations and leading marches intended to push for change. And like activism on behalf of gay and lesbian people, activism for the transgender community also focuses heavily on the legal system. Advocates work with lawmakers and in the courts to improve the lives of transgender Americans.

Gender Expression

The term *transgender* encompasses a variety of people and gender expressions. Some are people who are assigned one gender at birth but identify as a member of the opposite gender later in life. These people are often referred to as trans women (females who were assigned the male gender at birth) or trans men (males originally assigned the female gender). Some of the best-known transgender people in the United States have followed this route. Caitlyn Jenner, for example, was born Bruce Jenner in 1949. Bruce Jenner grew up identifying as male and became a star athlete who won the decathlon at the 1976 Olympic Games. In

In 2015 former decathlon-winning Olympian Bruce Jenner publicly announced that he identified as a woman and from that day forward would be known as Caitlyn Jenner (pictured).

2015, however, Jenner came out as a woman, adopting her new name and announcing that she would no longer live as a man.

Even within the world of trans men and trans women, there is plenty of variation. Some people do not come out as transgender until they are relatively old; Jenner did not announce that she was a woman until she was well past sixty. Others transition to their preferred gender as young adults, teenagers, or children. Many transgender people take hormones—typically estrogen for trans women and testosterone for trans men. Hormones modify their bodies to enhance the characteristics of their preferred gender. This could include a deeper voice for trans men and less facial hair for women. Some, but not all, undergo sexual reassignment surgery, in which their genitals are altered to match their gender.

And not all transgender people identify as either men or women. Some transgender Americans say they are nonbinary, gender

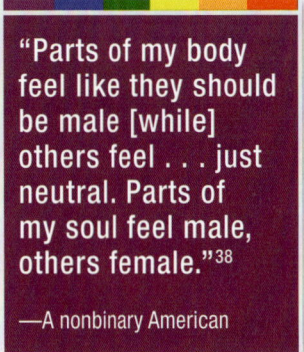

"Parts of my body feel like they should be male [while] others feel . . . just neutral. Parts of my soul feel male, others female."[38]

—A nonbinary American

nonconforming, or genderqueer—all terms that imply neither female nor male. People in this category argue that traditional ideas of gender simply do not apply to them. Some feel that they are neither male nor female. Some see themselves as a combination of the two. "Parts of my body feel like they should be male," reports one nonbinary person, while "others feel . . . just neutral. Parts of my soul feel male, others female."[38]

State and Local Policies

The United States has no overarching federal policy on transgender people. No national law specifically protects transgender people from discrimination. As a result, legal treatment of transgender people varies by state and sometimes even by municipality. As early as 2002, for example, New York City made it illegal to discriminate against people according to their status as transgender or gender nonconforming. Other large cities such as Phoenix, Arizona, and St. Louis, Missouri, have also enacted such laws. Many smaller cities have followed suit: in Pennsylvania, for example, several dozen municipalities have nondiscrimination laws on the books. About twenty states, too, have laws offering protections in housing, jobs, or other public accommodations for transgender people. These include Iowa, New Mexico, and Connecticut, among others.

At the same time, many other states and municipalities do not provide any antidiscrimination protection for the transgender community. Idaho, Oklahoma, and West Virginia are examples. The reasons for the refusal to enact antidiscrimination laws vary. When a nondiscrimination bill was proposed in 2018 in Cleveland, Ohio, for example, one opponent argued that the bill "tramples religious freedom."[39] This person argued that employers and landlords whose religions taught that gender was unchangeable would be forced to recognize the rights of people who had changed theirs. Whatever the reasons, a transgender person living in Bozeman, Montana; Fort Worth, Texas; or anywhere in Colorado has the same right to a job and an apartment as anyone else. This does not hold true in most of Mississippi and Nebraska, neither of which have laws protecting the rights of transgender individuals.

The effect of different laws can have other impacts on transgender Americans. In nearly all states, as of early 2020, people can get their birth certificates changed to reflect their preferred gender identity. In some states people wishing to change their

Transgender Athletes

One important controversy regarding transgender individuals is the role they should—or should not—play in sports. Much of the question revolves around whether girls' high school sports should allow participation by transgender athletes. For LGBTQ activists, the answer is easy: the athletes identify as female and should be permitted to take part. But for others, the answer is equally clear in the other direction. Transgender girls, they point out, often have strong builds and high levels of muscle mass. In this view, transgender athletes have an unfair physical advantage over non-transgender athletes.

A recent example of this controversy took place in Connecticut. Like many of its neighbors, the state had decided that transgender girls would be able to play sports on girls' teams at the high school level. Then, in 2017, two highly talented transgender runners—Andraya Yearwood and Terry Miller—joined the girls' track teams at their high schools. Yearwood and Miller soon were dominating their events.

Their success distressed several runners on track teams at other Connecticut high schools. They argued that they could not compete with transgender runners. In 2020 three Connecticut runners and their families sued in an attempt to keep transgender athletes from competing in girls' sports. Supported by the American Civil Liberties Union and other civil rights groups, the transgender runners continue to compete in girls' events as they await a ruling. "Because they don't want me to run," says Yearwood, "I have to run harder."

Quoted in Mirin Fader, "Andraya Yearwood Knows She Has the Right to Compete," Bleacher Report, December 17, 2018. https://bleacherreport.com.

gender on their birth records must first undergo sex reassignment surgery. However, two states—Tennessee and Ohio—do not allow birth certificates to be changed. As with nondiscrimination laws, the ability to get a revised birth certificate depends in large part on where people happen to live.

The struggle for transgender equality has therefore focused in large part on passing state and local laws designed to protect the rights of transgender people. The number of cities and states passing antidiscrimination laws continues to grow. The state of New York, for instance, passed a bill offering protections to its transgender residents in early 2019. "We are finally welcoming a fairer and more equal New York,"[40] said an activist. And other states and municipalities that do not currently offer protections

A transgender woman from Albuquerque, New Mexico, smiles after receiving a new birth certificate reflecting her gender change. As of early 2020 people in nearly all states can get their birth certificates changed to reflect their preferred gender identity.

may do so soon. In Michigan, for example, activists were hoping to place an antidiscrimination measure on the ballot in November 2020. By bringing the matter directly to the voters, advocates for a nondiscrimination law would bypass the Michigan legislature, which has refused to bring such a bill up for consideration.

Through the Courts

Much of the battle for transgender equality has taken place in the courts. In early 2020, for example, lawsuits were making their way through the courts in Ohio and Tennessee. The goal of those lawsuits was to force these states to allow changes to birth certificates. Similar cases had already succeeded in several other states. In Idaho, for example, a judge ruled that the state's refusal to change gender on birth certificates was a violation of the US Constitution. Allowing gender changes on birth certificates, the judge noted, "promotes the health, well-being, and safety of transgender people without impacting the rights of others."[41]

> "Male and female . . . fail to properly categorize a person like me. So I challenged that."[42]
>
> —Transgender activist Jamie Shupe

Many of the laws that have been put into place have been a direct result of work by transgender people themselves. In 2016, for example, Oregon resident Jamie Shupe, a nonbinary person who used the pronouns *they* and *them*, petitioned a state judge to allow them to list their gender as nonbinary rather than male or female on legal documents. Shupe requested support from several civil rights organizations, among them the LGBTQ advocacy group Lambda Legal. The organizations they contacted turned them down—an indication, perhaps, that even these organizations saw Shupe's case as unlikely to succeed. Nevertheless, the judge ruled in Shupe's favor, making them the first American to be officially identified as nonbinary. "Male and female . . . fail to properly categorize a person like me," Shupe said afterward. "So I challenged that."[42]

In other situations, the battle is to get discrimination recognized as such. Philecia Barnes, a transgender woman, was a police officer in Cincinnati, Ohio, when she applied to be promoted to sergeant. She passed the necessary exam but was ultimately denied a promotion. The city asserted that Barnes was not an effective police officer and would make a poor sergeant. But Barnes believed that the real reason the city turned her down had to do with her transgender status, and so she brought suit against the city in 2015. Supported by a Cincinnati sergeant who claimed that officials had decided to "target [Barnes] for failure,"[43] Barnes won the court case. Her case established that transgender individuals could win suits based on sex discrimination.

Other cases have sought to get businesses and government to adhere to existing laws. In 2015 Katherine Prescott of California took her fourteen-year-old transgender son, Kyler, to a San Diego hospital for mental health treatment. Though both Kyler and his mother told hospital staff that he identified as a boy, many staff

Laverne Cox: Transgender Actress and Activist

One of the best-known transgender Americans today is actress Laverne Cox, most famous for her role as Sophia Burset on the television show *Orange Is the New Black*. A native of Alabama, Cox has a strong background in the arts. She studied creative writing and dance at a specialized art school when she was a teenager. She attended college in Indiana and then in New York, and moved from writing and dance to acting.

Cox first came to the attention of the general public as a contestant on a reality show called *I Want to Work for Diddy*. That show led to Cox becoming a performer and producer of another show, a makeover series called *TRANSform Me*. Cox also had small roles on various other television shows before joining the cast of *Orange Is the New Black*. She has won accolades and awards for her presentation of her character, a transgender woman imprisoned for credit card fraud. Cox has a number of transgender firsts, including being the first openly transgender person to appear on the cover of *Time* magazine and the first to have a statue in London's famous wax museum Madame Tussauds. Her activism on behalf of the transgender community, especially women of color, has been much admired as well.

members referred to him as a girl and used female pronouns to describe him. "Honey, I would call you 'he,'" a staff member told Kyler at one point, "but you're such a pretty girl."[44] Kyler was released early from the hospital and died by suicide several weeks later. His mother sued, arguing that the hospital had ignored California law requiring appropriate treatment of transgender people. In 2016 the case was decided in her favor.

Bathroom Bills

Much of the controversy regarding transgender rights has centered on the issue of public bathrooms. Some bathrooms in stores, stadiums, and other public spaces are gender neutral—that is, they have a single toilet that can be used by either men or women. But many others are segregated by gender. Under these circumstances, it can be difficult for a transgender person to know whether to use a male- or female-designated bathroom. That is especially true for people who are just beginning their gender transition, who may feel like one gender but still look in many ways like a member of the other gender. It is also true for nonbinary people.

> "Intimate spaces should be safe spaces."[45]
>
> —A Texas parent

As a result of these concerns, transgender activists have lobbied for the right to use public bathrooms that correspond with their preferred gender. But in some parts of the United States, opposition to transgender people has coalesced around the fear that trans women might use women's bathrooms. In an effort to raise concern about this possibility, some people have distributed pictures showing large, burly men walking into women's restrooms. The idea, stated or not, is that women and girls will be unsafe if trans women are allowed to use women's restrooms. "Intimate spaces should be safe spaces,"[45] says one Texas parent worried about the security of women.

In North Carolina these concerns culminated in the passage of a so-called bathroom bill. The city of Charlotte had passed a

One controversial aspect of transgender rights is the issue of public bathrooms. In many facilities these bathrooms are gender neutral, meaning they have a single toilet that can be used by either men or women. But many others are segregated by gender.

law giving certain protections to transgender residents, including the right to use whichever bathroom best matched their preferred gender. Some people in the state strongly disapproved of the bill, and in 2016 governor Pat McCrory signed a bill that overrode the Charlotte ordinance. The bill went further, however, stating that people throughout the state would be required to use public bathrooms that matched their biological sex even if that conflicted with the gender with which they identified.

Controversy and Boycotts

The bill was controversial from the start. Transgender activists were furious. They pointed out that transgender people are much more likely to be victims of violence than to engage in it. They also argued that the law was discriminatory because it targeted only one group: transgender individuals. A number of national organizations agreed, and businesses began avoiding the state. The National Basketball Association, for example, was scheduled to have its All-Star game in Charlotte in 2017 but moved it elsewhere in solidarity with the state's transgender population.

Indeed, the bill ultimately proved unpopular even with many people in North Carolina. In late 2016 McCrory came up for re-election but lost to Roy Cooper, who opposed the bathroom bill. Many observers attributed McCrory's loss to his support of the law. As governor, Cooper succeeded in eliminating some of the most objectionable parts of the law. "We are thrilled to obtain some clarity and relief for transgender North Carolinians,"[46] said Irena Como, a lawyer with the American Civil Liberties Union. Still, many people disagree with Cooper's actions, and as a result, the controversy over bathrooms in North Carolina is not over.

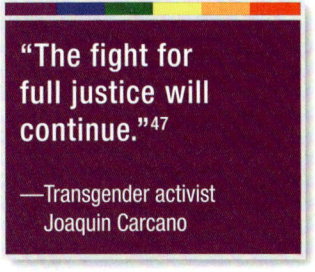

"The fight for full justice will continue."[47]

—Transgender activist Joaquin Carcano

The larger battle for transgender rights continues as well. Transgender activists have had some notable successes, such as the cases involving Shupe, Barnes, and Prescott. They have also had some difficult setbacks, including the passage of North Carolina's original bathroom bill, and many challenges remain. Still, advocates remain optimistic and look forward to a brighter future for transgender Americans. As activist Joaquin Carcano puts it, "The fight for full justice will continue."[47]

Chapter Five

Moving Forward

To some, the *Obergefell* decision felt like the end of the struggle for LGBTQ civil rights. In a relatively short period of time, the political landscape for LGBTQ people had shifted, apparently forever. They could adopt, join the military, marry, and much more. Gay people were starring in movies and performing as professional athletes. Baseball teams held Pride Nights; stores targeted gay couples and families in their advertising. There seemed to be few obstacles keeping lesbians and gay men from full participation in society. Indeed, more than one gay advocacy organization disbanded after the goal of marriage equality was achieved. "The mission was to get these policy objectives passed," said Norman C. Simon of one of these groups, the Empire State Pride Agenda, "and we feel we have done that."[48]

But in fact the battle was not won. In the years following the *Obergefell* decision, some of the rights earned by LGBTQ people appeared to be vulnerable. As of early 2020, activists feared that many of their hard-won rights were in danger of disappearing. Though a majority of Americans now support LGBTQ rights in areas such as marriage equality and the right of gay people to adopt children, resistance remains. Those who oppose rights for the LGBTQ community are a minority in many parts of the country, especially in the large urban areas of the Northeast and Pacific Coast. But they are not a minority in other regions. Backed by powerful politicians and by some religious leaders as well, the anti-LGBTQ forces remain influential in American life—and may one day succeed in rolling back some of the progress gained in the previous half century.

Anti-*Obergefell* Backlash

There was no shortage of enthusiasm for the *Obergefell* decision when it was handed down in 2015. But there was no shortage of dismay, either. "Gay marriage is legal now," mourned a Twitter user. "This country has turned away from God."[49] Much of the criticism rested on the notion that homosexuality was morally wrong and against religious teachings. Others couched their concerns in different ways. Three Supreme Court justices, for example, vigorously dissented from the majority opinion in the *Obergefell* case by making

As a sign of support for LGBTQ rights, baseball teams have held Pride Nights. Shown here are the mascots for the New York Mets, Mr. and Mrs. Met, who announced the team's Pride Night at a news conference.

the argument that laws should be made by legislatures, not by courts. Justice Antonin Scalia called the ruling a "threat to American democracy."[50]

Regardless of how people viewed the *Obergefell* decision, it was the law of the land. In most places, it was followed—but not everywhere. A handful of officials in a few states decided they would not issue marriage licenses to gay couples. In Alabama several judges empowered to issue marriage licenses decided they would no longer issue licenses to anyone. That was also the case in Kentucky, where issuing marriage licenses is the responsibility of county clerks—and where two of these clerks announced that they would not follow the law. One, Kim Davis, the clerk of Rowan County in the eastern part of the state, became a minor celebrity for her refusal. For religious reasons, Davis objected to same-sex marriage; like the judges in Alabama, she decided that she would issue no marriage licenses at all rather than feel forced to provide a license to a gay or lesbian couple. "It wasn't just a spur-of-the-moment decision," she says. "It was thought out, and I sought God on it."[51]

Several same-sex couples sued Davis, and Kentucky governor Steve Beshear ordered her to start providing marriage licenses again. However, Davis refused to change her stance. Davis and her supporters pointed out that same-sex couples could obtain a marriage license in nearly every other county in Kentucky, including several within a few dozen miles of the Rowan County courthouse. Her supporters noted as well that Davis's actions did not discriminate against same-sex couples; she had stopped issuing marriage licenses to all couples. Finally, Davis and her supporters argued that the Constitution guarantees religious freedom. In this view, Davis could not be required to do something she believed to be in opposition to the teachings of her faith.

Undermining Marriage Equality

LGBTQ advocates were not swayed by these arguments. "Telling people to go to another county is like saying, 'We don't want your kind of people here,'"[52] says one man who was turned down

Doubts About *Obergefell*

In his dissent from the *Obergefell* ruling, Justice John Roberts argued that even if marriage equality were a worthy goal, the question should have been settled through legislatures rather than through courts.

> Here and abroad, people are in the midst of a serious and thoughtful public debate on the issue of same-sex marriage. They see voters carefully considering same-sex marriage, casting ballots in favor or opposed, and sometimes changing their minds. They see political leaders similarly reexamining their positions, and either reversing course or explaining adherence to old convictions confirmed anew. They see governments and businesses modifying policies and practices with respect to same-sex couples, and participating actively in the civic discourse. They see countries overseas democratically accepting profound social change, or declining to do so. . . .
>
> When decisions are reached through democratic means, some people will inevitably be disappointed with the results. But those whose views do not prevail at least know that they have had their say. . . . But today the Court puts a stop to all that. By deciding this question under the Constitution, the Court removes it from the realm of democratic decision. There will be consequences to shutting down the political process on an issue of such profound public significance. Closing debate tends to close minds. People denied a voice are less likely to accept the ruling of a court on an issue that does not seem to be the sort of thing courts usually decide.

Obergefell v. Hodges, 135 S. Ct. 2584 (2015). www.supremecourt.gov.

by Davis when he and his partner applied for a marriage license. Advocates also pointed out that Davis's actions were certainly sparked by the *Obergefell* decision. Even though heterosexual couples also could not obtain marriage licenses in Rowan County, they noted, Davis's actions were based on antipathy toward gay people and same-sex marriage. And LGBTQ advocates suggested that if Davis believed herself unable to perform any part of her job, the correct response was not to refuse to carry out her responsibilities but to resign.

The situation attracted national attention, with several prominent leaders taking Davis's side. Republican presidential candidate Mike Huckabee went so far as to call Davis's treatment an example of the "criminalization of Christianity."[53] Davis eventually agreed to a compromise in which she would allow her deputy clerks to issue marriage licenses to straight and gay couples alike. Though Davis's opposition to same-sex marriage did not in the end carry the day, it did represent the depth of feeling against marriage equality among at least some Americans. Thus, for LGBTQ activists, the case serves as a warning that marriage equality may still be undermined in the United States.

There is other evidence, too, that same-sex marriage is under attack. Even before the *Obergefell* decision, the city of Houston, Texas, offered benefits to same-sex city employees. In 2013, though, the city was sued by two men who argued that taxpayers should not have to pay for these benefits. To LGBTQ activists, this argument seemed dangerous. In their opinion, the *Obergefell* decision, by guaranteeing the right of same-sex couples to marry, also guaranteed that same-sex couples should receive all the benefits enjoyed by married opposite-sex couples. They were distressed, then, when the Texas Supreme Court did not immediately decide the case in favor of the city, but rather returned the lawsuit to a lower court with instructions to determine the extent to which *Obergefell* applied. As of early 2020 the case was still in the court system. Clearly, a decision against the city would be a major blow to LGBTQ advocates. As activist Mark Joseph Stern puts it, "gay couples' right to equal marriage can never be taken for granted."[54]

> "Gay couples' right to equal marriage can never be taken for granted."[54]
>
> —LGBTQ activist Mark Joseph Stern

Religious Freedom

One of the issues raised in the Davis case involves religious freedom: Davis argued that her religious beliefs should have exempted her from issuing marriage licenses to gay and lesbian couples. On the face of it, this was a reasonable argument, since the United States has a long tradition of providing religious freedom to its citizens. "Congress shall make no law respecting an establishment of religion," reads the First Amendment to the US Constitution, "or prohibiting the free exercise thereof." And over the years, many Americans have used religious freedom as a reason to avoid engaging in activities they find morally wrong. Members of religions that oppose war, for instance, can qualify to be excused from military service based on their religious convictions.

In the case of Davis, the courts did not look favorably on her argument that her religious opposition to homosexuality exempted her from having to issue marriage licenses. In large part that was because Davis was a public official, so issuing marriage licenses was a central part of her job. "She doesn't get to pick and choose which of her duties she will perform,"[55] says law professor Katherine Franke. But government officials are not the only people who have claimed that their religious beliefs compel them to treat gay and lesbian people differently from others. Similar claims have been made (with some success) by people working in the private sector. The reality is that religious freedom arguments have become important weapons in the battle against LGBTQ rights.

In 2012, for example, Charlie Craig and David Mullins of Colorado ordered a custom wedding cake from a local bakery called the Masterpiece Cakeshop. The owner of the shop, Jack Phillips, declined to make the cake for the couple. His religious beliefs, Phillips explained, taught him that homosexuality was wrong. Though Craig and Mullins were welcome to buy any of the cakes already on display in the store, Phillips said, he would not bake them a custom-made cake. Craig and Mullins promptly complained to the Colorado Civil Rights Commission, pointing out that Colorado law prohibited discrimination on the basis of sexual orientation. The commission agreed with them, ordering Phillips to provide wedding cakes to gay couples as well as straight ones.

Jack Phillips, the owner of Masterpiece Cakeshop in Lakewood, Colorado, talks to reporters outside the US Supreme Court in Washington, DC. After refusing to custom-make a wedding cake for gay couple based on his religious beliefs, he was sued by the couple.

Phillips, however, refused. In an echo of the Davis case, he stopped providing wedding cakes to all customers, gay or straight. Phillips also brought the case to the Colorado Court of Appeals, repeating his claim that making a cake for a gay wedding would be an unacceptable infringement of his religious freedom. In another echo of Davis, he pointed out that there were many other bakeries in the area and that the couple had experienced no difficulty finding another bakery to make the cake they desired. In 2018 the case made its way to the US Supreme Court, where it was decided 7–2 in Phillips's favor.

The decision was a victory for Phillips, but the justices also cautioned that discrimination based on sexual orientation was not acceptable. As the decision put it, "these disputes must be resolved with tolerance, without undue disrespect to sincere religious beliefs, and without subjecting gay persons to indignities when they seek goods and services in an open market."[56] LGBTQ advocates worry that a similar case might result in a less favorable ruling from the Supreme Court, one that would enshrine religious freedom over the rights of gay and transgender Americans. "Anti-LGBT groups now have an even greener light to [argue] that it is legal to discriminate against LGBT people based on religious beliefs,"[57] writes a journalist.

Other Issues

Laws and practices in individual states continue to pose huge challenges for LGBTQ activists. These laws and practices deal with a wide array of issues. Laws that prevent teachers from discussing homosexuality—or at least, forbid teachers from mentioning it in a positive light—are one example. Alabama has such a law; it states that health and sex education classes "must emphasize . . . that homosexuality is not a lifestyle acceptable to the general public."[58] Not surprisingly, the LGBTQ community objects to this law and others like it and is working to eradicate them. Currently, six states (all in the South) have laws of this type.

Another concern for LGBTQ activists is the practice known as conversion therapy. Conversion therapy is a highly controversial type of counseling that aims to turn homosexual individuals into heterosexual individuals. Most evidence suggests that conversion therapy is ineffective; still, gay and lesbian adolescents often find themselves pushed into this type of therapy by their parents. Since conversion therapy is based on the idea that homosexuality is bad and heterosexuality is the only acceptable path, LGBTQ advocates would like to ban its use for minors. As of early 2020, nineteen states and a number of municipalities have done exactly that. But nationwide many minors continue to be forced into therapy they neither need nor want. Efforts continue to encourage more states to forbid this practice—or to have a ban that covers the nation as a whole.

These two issues point up perhaps the biggest concern for LGBTQ advocates: the lack of protections for LGBTQ individuals

Laws and practices in a number of states continue to pose challenges for LGBTQ individuals. One example is states with laws preventing teachers from discussing homosexuality, or at least forbidding them from mentioning it in a positive light.

on the federal level. No federal statute protects LGBTQ workers from being fired because of their sexuality or gender expression; no federal law ensures that LGBTQ renters cannot be evicted for the same reasons. And to be sure, workers do get fired for their sexuality or gender expression in states that lack these protections. Michigan resident Aimee Stephens, for example, was fired from a job at a funeral home after she came out as transgender. The protections enjoyed by a resident of Maryland or Washington do not translate to Michigan—or many other states.

A National Law

LGBTQ rights activists argue that national nondiscrimination laws are necessary to ensure that all LGBTQ individuals receive equal treatment—in commerce, work, education, housing, and all other aspects of daily life. Accordingly, lawmakers in Congress have introduced bills that would protect LGBTQ people in housing, jobs, and public accommodations. In 2019, for example, US representative David Cicilline of Rhode Island introduced in the House a bill known as the Equality Act. This bill was designed to amend existing civil rights laws to include sexual orientation and gender expression in addition to race, color, religion, and other traditionally protected classes.

The opposition to bills like the Equality Act is strong, however. Much of the opposition has come from religious organizations that teach that homosexuality is unnatural and not acceptable in

Conversion Therapy

Peter Cruz admitted to his priest that he was gay when he was seventeen. These are his recollections of his time in conversion therapy.

> I told the priest I'd do whatever he advised. It was then he suggested meeting with Joseph Nicolosi, the "father of conversion therapy," who I started to see regularly shortly thereafter. . . . I'm sad to say I am one of the nearly 700,000 LGBTQ adults in the United States who have been subjected to these harmful practices.
>
> At our initial meeting, Nicolosi described circumstances in a person's upbringing that leads one to "believe they are homosexual." Because I didn't have a strong male father figure to balance the close relationship I had with my mom, Nicolosi explained, I started to mirror her feminine characteristics. . . . To counter this, Nicolosi directed me to spend more time with my father. . . .
>
> Eventually, the tone of Nicolosi's sessions became more hostile. "You're not trying hard enough," he said. "If you choose this lifestyle, you're going to get AIDS and die." His words stuck with me, as if I only heard them yesterday.
>
> My relationship with Nicolosi became so tense that I eventually refused to speak during our sessions. . . . Feeling my distress, my mom finally suspended our sessions.
>
> I was traumatized by the whole experience. It led me down a path of severe depression, and at one point I attempted to take my own life.

Peter Cruz, "The 'Father of Conversion Therapy' Tried to Change My Sexual Orientation," Into, October 25, 2018. www.intomore.com.

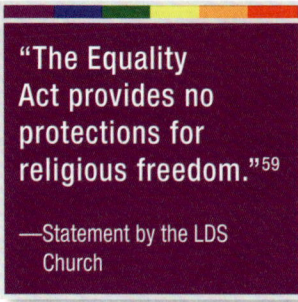

"The Equality Act provides no protections for religious freedom."[59]

—Statement by the LDS Church

the eyes of God. The United States Conference of Catholic Bishops, for example, opposed the Equality Act, fearing that it would interfere with the freedoms of speech and religion of Catholics and Catholic organizations. The Church of Jesus Christ of Latter-Day Saints (LDS), also known as the Mormons, has also weighed in against the bill for similar reasons. "While providing extremely broad protections for LGBT rights," reads a statement from LDS Church leaders, "the Equality Act provides no protections for religious freedom."[59]

"No American should be at risk of being fired, evicted from their home or denied services because of who they are or whom they love."[60]

—Wisconsin senator Tammy Baldwin

The list of organizations that support the Equality Act is also long, including the American Medical Association, the US Chamber of Commerce, and several religious organizations. But the support has not been enough to overcome the opposition, and so, like other laws before it, the Equality Act has faltered. It passed the US House in 2019, but as of early 2020 it was stalled in the Senate. It is not clear whether the bill will ever become law. Still, advocates press on. Regardless of the state they live in, says Wisconsin senator Tammy Baldwin, "no American should be at risk of being fired, evicted from their home or denied services because of who they are or whom they love."[60] Baldwin's words represent the core message of the struggle for LGBTQ rights, and that is the message advocates will continue to carry into the future.

Source Notes

Introduction: The LGBTQ Rights Movement

1. Quoted in Human Rights Campaign, "Transgender Military Service," October 1, 2019. www.hrc.org.
2. Barbara L. McAneny, "AMA Statement on Pentagon's Ban on Transgender in Military," American Medical Association, April 11, 2019. www.ama-assn.org.
3. Quoted in Hallie Jackson and Courtney Kube, "Trump's Controversial Transgender Military Policy Goes into Effect," NBC News, April 12, 2019. www.nbcnews.com.
4. Quoted in Katy Steinmetz, "Why Federal Laws Don't Explicitly Ban Discrimination Against LGBT Americans," *Time*, March 21, 2019. https://time.com.

Chapter One: Toward Tolerance

5. Quoted in Lillian Faderman, *The Gay Revolution*. New York: Simon and Schuster, 2015, p. 40.
6. Quoted in Patricia Cohen, "Concerns Beyond Just *Where the Wild Things Are*," *New York Times*, September 9, 2008. www.nytimes.com.
7. Quoted in Stephanie Buck, "Philadelphia's Largest Gay Hangout Denied Service to 150 People in 1965 for 'Looking Gay,'" Timeline, May 19, 2017. https://timeline.com.
8. Quoted in Hugh Ryan, "How Dressing in Drag Was Labeled a Crime in the 20th Century," History, June 25, 2019. www.history.com.
9. Quoted in David Carter, *Stonewall: The Riots That Sparked the Gay Revolution*. New York: Griffin, 2010, p. 148.
10. Quoted in Carter, *Stonewall*, p. 152.
11. Quoted in Carter, *Stonewall*, p. 198.
12. Quoted in Richard D. Lyons, "Psychiatrists, in a Shift, Declare Homosexuality No Mental Illness," *New York Times*, December 16, 1973. www.nytimes.com.
13. Quoted in Lyons, "Psychiatrists, in a Shift, Declare Homosexuality No Mental Illness."

14. Quoted in William Grimes, "Alfred Freedman; Led Effort to Reclassify Homosexuality," *Boston Globe*, April 22, 2011. http://archive.boston.com.
15. Quoted in Iver Peterson, "Homosexuals Gain Support on Campus," *New York Times*, June 5, 1974. www.nytimes.com.
16. Quoted in Dudley Clendinen and Adam Nagourney, *Out for Good: The Struggle to Build a Gay Rights Movement in America*. New York: Simon and Schuster, 2001, p. 301.
17. Quoted in B. Drummond Ayres Jr., "Miami Votes 2 to 1 to Repeal Law Barring Bias Against Homosexuals," *New York Times*, June 8, 1977. www.nytimes.com.
18. Quoted in Andrew Hartman, *A War for the Soul of America*, 2nd ed. Chicago: University of Chicago, 2016, p. 95.

Chapter Two: The AIDS Crisis

19. Trevor Martin, "Facing My Fear," *The Guardian* (Manchester), April 15, 2016. www.theguardian.com.
20. Quoted in Kelsey Louie, "Fear Is a Plague, Education the Cure," *New York Daily News*, October 18, 2014. www.nydailynews.com.
21. Quoted in Maria L. LaGanga, "The First Lady Who Looked Away," *The Guardian* (Manchester), March 11, 2016. www.theguardian.com.
22. Quoted in Dennis Hevesi, "Rodger McFarlane; Early AIDS Activist Led Key Organizations," *San Diego (CA) Union-Tribune*, May 24, 2009. www.sandiegouniontribune.com.
23. Quoted in New York Lesbian & Gay Experimental Film Festival, *ACT Up Oral History Project*. New York: New York Lesbian & Gay Experimental Film Festival, 2004. www.actuporalhistory.org.
24. Quoted in Raymond Smith and Donald P. Haider-Markel, *Gay and Lesbian Americans and Political Participation: A Reference Handbook*. Santa Barbara, CA: ABC-CLIO, 2002, p. 47.
25. Quoted in NYC LGBT Historic Sites Project, "ACT UP: Demonstrations on Wall Street," 2017. www.nyclgbtsites.org.
26. Quoted in Michael Specter, "Public Nuisance," *New Yorker*, May 6, 2002. www.newyorker.com.

27. German Lopez, "The Reagan Administration's Unbelievable Response to the HIV/AIDS Epidemic," Vox, December 1, 2015. www.vox.com.
28. *Newsweek*, "The End of AIDS?," December 1, 1996. www.newsweek.com.

Chapter Three: The Struggle for Acceptance

29. Quoted in US General Accounting Office, "Homosexuals in the Armed Service: United States GAO Report," Fordham University, January 2, 2020. https://sourcebooks.fordham.edu.
30. Quoted in Carl Matthes, "Defending LGBT Gains: Voting For, Not Against," LA Progressive, May 9, 2016. www.laprogressive.com.
31. Quoted in *New York Times*, "The Supreme Court," June 27, 2003. www.nytimes.com.
32. Quoted in Betsy Swan, "Jeb Bush's War on Gay Adoption," Daily Beast, May 22, 2015. www.thedailybeast.com.
33. Quoted in Swan, "Jeb Bush's War on Gay Adoption."
34. GLAD, "*Pavan v. Smith*," 2020. www.glad.org.
35. Quoted in John-Henry Perera, "Politicians Who Changed Their View of Same-Sex Marriage," *Albany (NY) Times Union*, July 2, 2015. www.timesunion.com.
36. Quoted in Amy Davidson Sorkin, "The Supreme Court Reaffirms Marriage Vows," *New Yorker*, June 26, 2015. www.newyorker.com.

Chapter Four: Transgender Issues

37. Quoted in Elizabeth F. Schwartz, "The Many Faces of Transgender Discrimination," *Trial*, American Association for Justice, October 2016. www.justice.org.
38. Quoted in Vera Papisova, "Here's What It Means When You Don't Identify as a Girl or a Boy," *Teen Vogue*, February 12, 2016. www.teenvogue.com.
39. Quoted in Courtney Astolfi, "Cuyahoga County Council Passes Anti-Discrimination Protections for LGBTQ Community," Cleveland.com, January 29, 2019. www.cleveland.com.

40. Quoted in Samantha Allen, "New York Passes Historic Transgender Anti-Discrimination Law," *Daily Beast*, January 15, 2019. www.thedailybeast.com.
41. F.V. v. Barron, 1:17-CV-00170-CWD (D. Idaho 2018). www.lambdalegal.org.
42. Quoted in Mary Emily O'Hara, "'Nonbinary' Is Now a Legal Gender, Oregon Court Rules," *Daily Dot*, June 10, 2016. www.dailydot.com.
43. Quoted in Philecia Barnes v. City of Cincinnati, 401 F.3d 729 (6th Cir. 2005). https://law.justia.com.
44. Quoted in Prescott v. Rady, 265 F. Supp. 3d 1090 (Dist. Court, S.D. California, 2017). www.courthousenews.com.
45. Quoted in Alexa Ura and Emma Platoff, "Senate Committee Passes 'Bathroom Bill' After 10 Hours of Testimony," *Texas Tribune*, July 21, 2017. www.texastribune.org.
46. Quoted in Merrit Kennedy, "North Carolina Reaches Settlement in Long Battle Over Bathrooms and Gender Identity," NPR, July 23, 2019. www.npr.org.
47. Quoted in Kennedy, "North Carolina Reaches Settlement in Long Battle Over Bathrooms and Gender Identity."

Chapter Five: Moving Forward

48. Quoted in Jesse McKinley, "Empire State Pride Agenda to Disband, Citing Fulfillment of Its Mission," *New York Times*, December 12, 2015. www.nytimes.com.
49. Quoted in Michael Pearson et al., "Here's How America Reacted to Friday's Marriage Equality Ruling," CNN, June 26, 2015. www.cnn.com.
50. Obergefell v. Hodges, 135 S. Ct. 2584 (2015). www.supremecourt.gov.
51. Quoted in Mike Wynn, "Clerk 'Sought God' on Marriage Licenses," *Louisville (KY) Courier-Journal*, July 21, 2015. www.courier-journal.com.
52. Quoted in Sheryl Gay Stolberg, "Kentucky Clerk Defies Court on Marriage Licenses for Gay Couples," *New York Times*, August 14, 2015. www.nytimes.com.

53. Quoted in Associated Press, "Huckabee Says Jailed Kentucky Clerk Shows 'Criminalization of Christianity,'" *New York Post*, September 4, 2015. https://nypost.com.
54. Mark Joseph Stern, "Alaska's Discrimination Against a Gay Couple Shows the Continued Threats to Marriage Equality," Slate, November 22, 2019. https://slate.com.
55. Quoted in Stolberg, "Kentucky Clerk Defies Court on Marriage Licenses for Gay Couples."
56. Quoted in Robert Barnes, "Supreme Court Rules in Favor of Baker Who Would Not Make Wedding Cake for Gay Couple," *Washington Post*, June 4, 2018. www.washingtonpost.com.
57. Samantha Allen, "These Five Court Cases Could Change the Future of LGBT Rights," Daily Beast, July 7, 2018. www.thedailybeast.com.
58. Quoted in "'No Promo Homo' Laws," GLSEN, 2019. www.glsen.org.
59. Quoted in Thomas Burr, "LDS Church Comes Out Against Equality Act, Saying LGBTQ Rights Bill Doesn't Ensure Religious Freedom," *Salt Lake Tribune* (Salt Lake City, UT), May 13, 2019. www.sltrib.com.
60. Quoted in Tim Fitzsimons, "Trump Opposes Federal LGBTQ Nondiscrimination Bill, Citing 'Poison Pills,'" NBC News, May 14, 2019. www.nbcnews.com.

A Time Line of LGBTQ Rights and Activism

1969
The Stonewall rebellion starts the LGBTQ movement.

1973
The American Psychiatric Association removes homosexuality from its list of mental illnesses.

1974
Kathy Kozachenko becomes the first openly gay American to win a political election.

1979
About one hundred thousand people march for gay rights in Washington, DC.

1983
Lambda Legal, a gay rights group, wins the first AIDS discrimination case.

1987
ACT UP is founded by Larry Kramer and others.

1993
Don't Ask, Don't Tell is signed into law.

1996
President Bill Clinton signs the Defense of Marriage Act.

2002
New York City bans discrimination against transgender people.

2003
Massachusetts courts legalize same-sex marriage; US Supreme Court legalizes gay sex in *Lawrence v. Texas*.

2011
Don't Ask, Don't Tell is repealed.

2015
Obergefell v. Hodges is decided, making marriage equality the law in all states.

2016
North Carolina passes a so-called bathroom bill.

2019
The Supreme Court allows the Trump administration to keep most transgender people from serving in the military.

The Equality Act passes the US House of Representatives.

Organizations and Websites

AIDS Coalition to Unleash Power (ACT UP)
https://actupny.org

ACT UP was an influential organization of the 1980s, when it used various tactics to call attention to the HIV/AIDS epidemic. The organization still exists today and lobbies on behalf of AIDS patients.

American Civil Liberties Union (ACLU)
www.aclu.org

The ACLU is one of the most famous and successful civil rights organizations in the United States. Along with taking on cases of prisoners' rights, free speech, and immigrant rights, the ACLU takes a deep interest in issues involving LGBTQ rights.

GLBTQ Legal Advocates & Defenders (GLAD)
www.glad.org

GLAD is a civil rights organization that offers legal services for LGBTQ individuals in New England and beyond. It especially represents transgender people and people living with HIV.

Human Rights Campaign
www.hrc.org

The Human Rights Campaign is a civil rights group dedicated to ensuring that LGBTQ people have the rights to which they are entitled. The organization works with lawyers, political leaders, and the media to achieve its goals.

Human Rights Watch
www.hrw.org

Human Rights Watch is an international organization that calls attention to violations of various rights worldwide. One of its focuses is the rights of LGBTQ people.

Lambda Legal

https://lambdalegal.org

Lambda Legal offers legal help for LGBTQ people. It has been involved in many high-profile civil rights cases focusing on transgender people, lesbians and gay men, and people living with HIV.

National Center for Transgender Equality

https://transequality.org

One of the best-known organizations working on behalf of transgender people, this organization lobbies political leaders to improve conditions for transgender individuals. It also works with the media to draw attention to transgender issues.

PFLAG

https://pflag.org

PFLAG was founded as a group made up of parents and friends of LGBTQ people. It offers support for those close to LGBTQ individuals and provides educational materials as well. Its focus is more on those around the LGBTQ person than on the LGBTQ individuals themselves.

For Further Research

Books

Heidi C. Feldman, *LGBT Discrimination*. San Diego, CA: ReferencePoint, 2019.

Jeremiah J. Garretson, *The Path to Gay Rights*. New York: New York University Press, 2018.

Susan Gluck Mezey, *Transgender Rights: From Obama to Trump*. New York: Routledge, 2019.

Gayle E. Pitman, *The Stonewall Riots*. New York: Abrams, 2019.

Pat Rarus, *The LGBT Rights Movement*. San Diego, CA: ReferencePoint, 2019.

Matthew Riemer and Leighton Brown, *We Are Everywhere: Protest, Power, and Pride in the History of Queer Liberation*. New York: Ten Speed, 2019.

Eric Rosswood and Kathleen Archambault, *We Make It Better: The LGBTQ Community and Their Positive Contributions to Society*. Coral Gables, FL: Mango, 2019.

Internet Sources

Lucas Acosta, "One Year Out: What's at Stake for LGBTQ Americans in 2020," Human Rights Campaign, November 3, 2019. www.hrc.org.

Samantha Allen, "These Five Court Cases Could Change the Future of LGBT Rights," Daily Beast, July 7, 2018. www.thedailybeast.com.

Human Rights Campaign, "Transgender Military Service," October 1, 2019. www.hrc.org.

Susan Miller, "Progress Toward LGBTQ Equality 'Is a Jagged Line.' Here's What Has Changed Over the Past Decade," *USA Today*, February 11, 2020. www.usatoday.com.

Obergefell v. Hodges, 135 S. Ct. 2584 (2015). www.supremecourt.gov.

Katy Steinmetz, "Why Federal Laws Don't Explicitly Ban Discrimination Against LGBT Americans," *Time*, March 21, 2019. https://time.com.

Index

Note: Boldface page numbers indicate illustrations.

Abzug, Bella, 16
adoption, 34–37, **36**
advocacy organizations
  American Civil Liberties Union
    basic facts about, 70
    North Carolina bathroom bill and, 51
    transgender athletes and, 45
    transgender individuals in military and, 7
  conversion therapy and, 59
  Daughters of Bilitis, 11
  discriminatory policies in states and localities, 59–60, **60**
  Gay Liberation Front (GLF), 14
  Gay Men's Health Crisis (GMHC), 22–24
  GLAD, 70
  Human Rights Campaign, 7, 70
  Human Rights Watch, 70
  Lambda Legal
    basic facts about, 71
    Lawrence v. Texas, 33–34, 35
    transgender individuals and, 47
  Mattachine Society, 11
  National Center for Transgender Equality, 42, 71
  National Gay Task Force, 15
  PFLAG, 71
  See also AIDS Coalition to Unleash Power (ACT UP)
AIDS (acquired immune deficiency syndrome), **20**
  activism and, 20
  appearance of, 19
  connection with homosexuality, 19
  death toll, 19
  demonization of homosexuals and hostility toward patients, 20, 21–22
  drug to treat, 26–27
  employment and, 22
  federal government response, 27–28
  Kaposi's sarcoma and, 21, 23
  PCP and, 21
  qualification as disability, 28
  spread of, 21
  in transgender individuals, 42
  treatments for, 26, 29
AIDS Coalition to Unleash Power (ACT UP)
  basic facts about, 70
  demands of, 24–25
  formation of, 24
  importance of, 29
  protests by, **25**, 25–27
  Stonewall compared to, 26
Alabama, 54, 59
American Civil Liberties Union
  basic facts about, 70
  North Carolina bathroom bill, 51
  transgender athletes and, 45
  transgender individuals in military and, 7
American Medical Association, 6, 62
American Psychiatric Association (APA), 8, 13–14, 15
Americans with Disabilities Act (ADA, 1990), 28
anti-sodomy laws, 33–34, 35
Arkansas, 37
Askew, Reubin, 16
athletes, transgender individuals as, 45

Baldwin, Tammy, 62
Barnes, Philecia, 47–48
bathroom bills, 49–51, **50**
Beshear, Steve, 54
bisexual, definition of, 6
Bowers, Geoffrey, 22
Bozeman, Montana, 45
Bryant, Anita, 16–17, 18
Buchanan, Patrick, 21
Bunch, Kenneth, 22
Bush, Jeb, 34

California, 17, 38
Carcano, Joaquin, 51
Charlotte, North Carolina, 49–50, 51
children
   adoption of, 34–37, **36**
   taken from homosexuals, 8
Church of Jesus Christ of Latter-Day Saints (LDS), 62
Cicilline, David, 60–61
Clinton, Bill, 31–33, 37
clothing, 10
colleges, **15**, 15–16
Colorado, 45, 57–59, **58**
Como, Irena, 51
Connecticut, 38, 44, 45
Constitution
   federal system, 35
   right to privacy, 33–34
conversion therapy, 59, 61
Cooper, Roy, 51
Cox, Laverne, 48
Craig, Charlie, 57–59
Cruz, Peter, 61
Crystal, Billy, 16

Dade County, Florida, 16–17
Daughters of Bilitis, 11
Davis, Kim, 54–57
Defense of Marriage Act (DOMA, 1996), 37, 39
Democratic Party and DADT, 33

Don't Ask, Don't Tell policy (DADT), 31–33

education, 22, 59
employment
   AIDS and, 22
   Dade County ban on discrimination, 16–17
   discrimination against homosexuals, 8, 60
   discrimination against transgender individuals, 42, 47–48
Equality Act (bill), 61

federal government
   absence of anti-discrimination laws, 59–61
   federalist system established by Constitution, 35
   response to AIDS of, 27–28
   advocacy organizations, 29
Florida
   adoption by homosexuals, **36**, 36–37
   Dade County anti-discrimination ordinance, 16–17
   number of homosexual teachers fired (1957-1963), 8
Fort Worth, Texas, 45
Franke, Katherine, 57
Friedman-Kien, Alvin, 23

Garner, Tyron, 33–34
gay, definition of, 6
gay bars, 10–11, **12**, 12–13
Gay Liberation Front (GLF), 14
Gay Men's Health Crisis (GMHC), 22–24
gender nonconforming individuals, 43–44
genderqueer individuals, 44
Ginsberg, Allen, 13
Ginsberg, Paul, 16

GLBTQ Legal Advocates & Defenders (GLAD), 70

Hawaii, 37, 38
health of transgender individuals, 42, 48–49
history
  before 1960s
    gay bars, 10–11
    homosexuality as mental disorder, 8
    organizations fighting for LGBTQ rights, 11
    "passing" by homosexuals, 9–10
    public opinion about, 9, **9**
    Stonewall, **12**, 12–13, 26, 30
  1970s
    antidiscrimination ordinances, 16–18
    APA removal of homosexuality from list of mental disorders, 13, 15
    APA support of civil rights for homosexuals, 13–14
    appearance of AIDS, 19
    increase in visibility of homosexuals, 15, **15**
  1980s–early 1990s
    activism, 20, 22–27, **25**
    AIDS, 19–27, **25**
HIV (human immunodeficiency virus), 21, 29
homosexuals, indicators of mainstream acceptance of, 41, 52, **53**
housing discrimination
  AIDS and, 22
  Dade County ban on, 16–17
  transgender individuals, 42
Houston, Texas, 56
Huckabee, Mike, 56
human immunodeficiency virus (HIV), 21, 29

Human Rights Campaign, 7, 70
Human Rights Watch, 70

Idaho, 44, 47
Iowa, 38, 44

Jenner, Caitlyn (Bruce), 42–43, **43**

Kaposi's sarcoma, 21, 23
Keisling, Mara, 7
Kennedy, Anthony, 34
Kentucky, 54–56
Kozachenko, Kathy, 15
Kramer, Larry
  founding of ACT UP, 24
  GMHC and, 23
  on need for confrontation, 26
  protest at St. Patrick's Cathedral (New York City), 27

Lambda Legal
  basic facts about, 71
  Lawrence v. Texas, 33–34, 35
  transgender individuals and, 47
Lawrence, John, 33–34
Lawrence v. Texas (2003), 33–34, 35
legal system
  anti-sodomy laws, 33–34, 35
  lawsuits to allow adoption by homosexuals, 36–37
  military policy, 31–33, **32**
  same-sex marriage Supreme Court decision, 35, 39–40
  state and local policies and court decisions
    bathroom use, 49–51, **50**
    benefits to same-sex city employees, 56
    existing discriminatory, 59
    same-sex marriage, 37, 38
    transgender individuals and, 44–49, **46**

strategy of advocacy organizations, 30–31
lesbian, definition of, 6
LGBTQ, meaning of term, 6

Maine, 38
Martin, Trevor, 19
Massachusetts, 38
Masterpiece Cakeshop, 57–59, **58**
Matlovich, Leonard, 16
Mattachine Society, 11
McCrory, Pat, 50, 51
Michigan, 47, 60
military
    homosexuals in, 16, 31–33, **32**
    transgender individuals in, 4–7, **5**
Milk, Harvey, 15
Miller, Terry, 45
Mississippi, 45
Mormons, 62
Moscone, George, 15
Mullins, David, 57–59

National Basketball Association, 51
National Center for Transgender Equality, 42, 71
National Gay Task Force, 15
Nebraska, 45
New Hampshire, 38
New Mexico, 44
Newsom, Gavin, 38
Newsweek (magazine), 29
New York (state), 38, 46
New York City, 26, 27, 44
New York Stock Exchange, 26
Nicolosi, Joseph, 61
nonbinary individuals, 43, 47
North Carolina, 49–51

Obama, Barack
    DADT and, 33
    DOMA and, 39
    transgender individuals in military and, 4
Obergefell v. Hodges
    background, 39–40
    backlash to decision, 53–56
    decision, 35, 40
    dissenting opinion, 53–54, 55
    gay reaction to decision, 39
Obergefell v. Kasich, 39
    See also Obergefell v. Hodges
Ohio, transgender individuals in, 44, 46, 47
Oklahoma, 44

PCP, 21
Pennsylvania, 44
PFLAG, basic facts about, 71
Phillips, Jack, 57–59, **58**
Phoenix, Arizona, 44
Prescott, Katherine, 48–49
Prescott, Kyler, 48–49
privacy rights, 33
psychological disorder of homosexuality, 8
public opinion
    adoption by homosexual couples, 35
    indicators of mainstream acceptance of homosexuals, 41, 52, **53**
    strongly anti-homosexuality, 9, **9**
    transgender individuals in military, 5

queer, definition of, 6

Reagan, Ronald, 27–28, **28**
religion
    anti-discrimination laws and, 61–62
    backlash to same-sex marriage and, 53, 54, 56–59, **58**
    homosexuals and, 17, 27

transgender individuals and, 44
Ringling Brothers and Barnum & Bailey Circus benefit, 24
Roberts, John, 55
Roman Catholic Church, 27, 62

same-sex marriage, **38**
    conducted by government officials, 38
    as illegal, 8, 37, 39
    as legal in some states, 37, 38
    religion and, 53, 54, 56–57, 56–59, **58**
    thought of as impossible, 14
    See also *Obergefell v. Hodges*
Scalia, Antonin, 54
Seattle, Washington, 17
Sendak, Maurice, 10
Shack, Ruth, 17
Shupe, Jamie, 47
Speakes, Larry, 27
sports, transgender individuals in, 45
St. Louis, Missouri, 44
Stephens, Aimee, 60
Stern, Mark Joseph, 56
Stonewall Inn, **12**
    gay activism and, 26
    purpose of rebellion, 30
    rebellion described, **12**, 12–13
suicide, 41, 49
Supreme Court
    adoption decision, 37
    anti-sodomy laws, 33–34, 35
    discrimination by private businesses on based on sexual orientation, 58–59
    same-sex marriage decision background, 39–40
    backlash to decision, 53–56
    decision, 35, 40
    dissenting opinion, 53–54, 55
    gay reaction to decision, 39

teenage transgender individuals and suicide, 41, 49
Tennessee, transgender individuals in, 46, 47
Texas, 33–34, 45, 56
transgender, definition of, 6, 41, 42
transgender individuals
    coming out by, 43
    famous, 42–43, **43**, 48
    health of, 42, 48–49
    hormonal and surgical treatments for, 43
    identification of, 43–44
    legal system and
        bathroom bills, 49–51, **50**
        birth certificates, 45–46, **46**, 47
        state and local policies, 44–47, **46**
    military service and, 4–7, **5**
    murder rate of, 42
    poverty of, 42
    in sports, 45
    suicide and, 41, 49
Trump, Donald, 5, **5**

United States Conference of Catholic Bishops, 62
US Chamber of Commerce, 62

Vermont, 38

West, Jason, 38
West Virginia, 44
White, Ryan, 22

Yearwood, Andraya, 45

Picture Credits

Cover: Stuart Monk/Shutterstock.com

5: Evan El-Amin/Shutterstock.com
9: Associated Press
12: Littleny/iStock
15: FatCamera/iStock
20: Associated Press
25: Mark Reinstein/Shutterstock.com
28: Mark Reinstein/Shutterstock.com
32: Bumble Dee/Shutterstock.com
36: wavebreakmedia/Shutterstock.com
38: CREATISTA/Shutterstock.com
43: JSTone/Shutterstock.com
46: Eddie Moore/ZUMA Press/Newscom
50: Gerry Matthews/Shutterstock.com
53: Associated Press
58: Jerome460/Shutterstock.com
60: monkeybusinessimages/iStock

About the Author

Stephen Currie is the author of dozens of books for young adults and children, many of them for ReferencePoint Press. He has also written textbooks, teacher guides, and other curriculum materials, and he has taught levels ranging from kindergarten through college. He lives with his family in New York's Hudson Valley.